area in which mainly he worked out his method in theology. He comments on Lonergan's enduring involvement with and contribution to trinitarian theology as itself a topic of the greatest importance within theology. He suggests some reasons why Lonergan has been so far unwilling to release for publication in translation any more than this one part of *De Deo Trino*, and why he has released even as much as he has.

BERNARD J. F. LONERGAN, a member of the Society of Jesus for over half a century and a priest since 1936, has received world recognition for his scholarly thought and writings. He is Research Professor at Regis College, a Jesuit seminary near Toronto. He also taught at the Divinity School, Harvard University. He is author of several influential books, including *Philosophy of God, and Theology* and *A Second Collection* (see back of jacket).

CONN O'DONOVAN is a member of the Faculty of Philosophy, The Institute of Philosophy and Theology, Dublin.

THE WAY TO NICEA

BOOKS BY
BERNARD LONERGAN

Published by The Westminster Press

The Way to Nicea:
The Dialectical Development of Trinitarian Theology

A Second Collection

Philosophy of God, and Theology

THE WAY TO NICEA

The Dialectical Development
of Trinitarian Theology

A translation by Conn O'Donovan from the
first part of *De Deo Trino*

BERNARD LONERGAN

THE WESTMINSTER PRESS
Philadelphia

This translation © copyright 1976 by Bernard Lonergan
and Conn O'Donovan is a translation of pages 17-112,
Pars Dogmatica, of *De Deo Trino,* Rome,
Gregorian University Press, 1964

PUBLISHED BY THE WESTMINSTER PRESS
Philadelphia, Pennsylvania ®

PRINTED IN THE UNITED STATES OF AMERICA

Library of Congress Cataloging in Publication Data

Lonergan, Bernard J   F
    The way to Nicea.

    "A translation of pages 17-112, Pars dogmatica, of De
Deo Trino, Rome, Gregorian University Press, 1964."
    Includes index.
    1. Trinity — History of doctrines. 2. Dogma,
Development of. 3. Sects. I. Title.
BT109.L6613   231   76-20792
ISBN 0-664-21340-5

CONTENTS

FOREWORD

In a recent study of "Biblical Hermeneutics" published in *Semeia*, Paul Ricoeur not only conceived live metaphor as creative expression but also attributed a similar power to parable, proverb, and apocalyptic.[1] So with his customary subtlety and finesse he brought to light how the gospels succeeded in taking us beyond the pedestrian confines of ordinary language and into the realm of religious meaning.

As there is live as well as dead metaphor, so too there is live as well as dead religion. Again, as creativity is discerned in the emergence of a religion, so too creativity is to be acknowledged in its vital acceptance, in living it day by day, in bringing about the adjustments to cultural variation and changing circumstance that the very vitality of a religion demands. So it is, as Wilfred Cantwell Smith remarked, that "All religions are new religions, every morning. For religions do not exist in the sky somewhere elaborated, finished, and static; they exist in men's hearts."[2]

With such creative vitality, its risks and its dangers, we have to do when we take for granted the distinction between writings included in the canonical scriptures and the broad spectrum of other writings, contemporary or subsequent, approved or suspected or rejected. But in the early Christian centuries further factors were involved. Besides the archaic style of Jewish Chris-

[1] *Semeia: An Experimental Journal for Biblical Criticism*, published irregularly by Scholars Press, University of Montana, Missoula, Montana 59801.
[2] Quoted by Walter Conn, *Studies in Religion/Sciences religieuses*, 5/3, Winter 1975, p. 222.

tian writers and the fantasy of Gnostics there was a puzzling undertow, a concern for clarity and coherence, that was destined eventually to add to the ordinary language of the bazaars and to the religious language of the gospels the incipient theological language of the Greek councils.

It is with this movement that these pages are concerned. But the reader must be warned that we do not propose to add to erudition by research, or to clarify interpretation by study, or to enrich history with fresh information. Such functional specialities we presuppose. Our purpose is to move on to a fourth, to a dialectic that, like an X-ray, sets certain key issues in high relief to concentrate on their oppositions and their interplay.

The reason for this procedure, which to an outsider might appear not only jejune but also violent, is that ante-Nicene thought was propelled by two distinct though related determinants. The explicit issue was christological, and to this the major writers explicitly adverted. But underpinning it and going forward without any explicit advertence on anyone's part, there was a far profounder matter: the emergence and the development of dogma, which began indeed at Nicea but continued down the centuries.

So it is that the christological thought of Tertullian, of Origen, of Athanasius, is to be studied on the basis of the explicit statements of these writers and in the context of the explicit Christian tradition. But if one would understand the long-term outcome of their thinking, an outcome they did not intend or desire, then the appropriate tool seems to be some type of dialectical analysis.

Bernard Lonergan
April, 1976.

TRANSLATOR'S INTRODUCTION

What is offered here is an English translation of the first part of the first volume of Bernard Lonergan's *De Deo Trino*.[1]

For those who are already very familiar with Father Lonergan's work so much might suffice as an introduction. However, having been encouraged to think that there may be many potential readers who would welcome further explanation, I shall

(1) survey the content and indicate the structure of the whole two-volume work of which the part translated constitutes about one sixth,

(2) give an account of Lonergan's academic courses on the Trinity, from 1945 to 1964, with some reference to other work in progress at the time of these courses,

(3) give a brief history of Lonergan's writings on the Trinity during his years in Rome culminating in the 1964 *De Deo Trino,*

(4) discuss the importance for Lonergan of trinitarian theo-

[1] *De Deo Trino* I: *Pars dogmatica.* II: *Pars systematica.* Gregorian University, 1964, pp. 308 and 321.

There may possibly be some readers who will wonder why Lonergan wrote the work in Latin in the first place. The explanation is that only within the last ten years has the rule gone out of force that obliged professors of theology and philosophy in Roman Catholic faculties and seminaries to teach all major courses through the medium of Latin, and *De Deo Trino* was composed originally as an aid to students of theology at the Gregorian University in Rome. Incidentally, Lonergan's students at the Gregorian came from some seventy nations.

logy as the area in which (mainly) he worked out his method in theology,

(5) comment on Lonergan's enduring involvement with and contribution to trinitarian theology as itself a topic of the greatest importance within theology,

(6) suggest some reasons why Lonergan has been so far unwilling to release for publication in translation any more than this one part of *De Deo Trino* and why he has released even as much as he has,

(7) make a few comments on the task of translation itself. The first part of *De Deo Trino*, sub-titled, *Dogmatic part*, opens with a brief preface, to which I shall refer again later.[2] This is followed by a ten-page introduction, in which Lonergan distinguishes between the aim, the proper object and the method of dogmatic theology, on the one hand, and on the other, the aim, the proper object and the method of positive theology in the strict sense. Dogmatic theology, the task on which he will be engaged in this first of the two volumes, "sets forth the dogmas of the Church and relates them to their origins in the sources of revelation",[3] whereas positive theology is concerned primarily not with the beliefs that are shared by significant authors, but with a precise, detailed understanding of those authors as individual, with their particular backgrounds, temperaments, interests, aims, manner and style of writing, and so on. The positive scholar is of course interested in content, but he also wants, for example, "to get right inside both Paul and John, in order to show how much they differ from each other in character and cast of mind";[4] the dogmatic theologian, on the other hand, "is so intent on grasping the content of what is said, that for him understanding the mentality and style of a particular author is not an end in itself, but rather the starting point from which he can proceed towards his own proper end".[5] Yet

[2] Below, p. xvii.
[3] *De Deo Trino*, I, p. 5.
[4] *Ibid.*, p. 10.
[5] *Ibid.*

though he must focus on what is common rather than on what is particular (common beliefs of Christians, which achieved the status of dogma, rather than the particular views of individual Christian authors), the dogmatic theologian must not snatch doctrines out of their historical context, to consider them in the abstract, as if they had a setting all of their own. "Too many students have been misled into believing that, by some kind of mysterious intuition, they can see at once in scripture something which emerged originally only with the passage of time and with great labour; something which many resisted and many denied; something which it took great minds to grasp, and which only gradually received acceptance in the Church".[6] The approach must be concrete; indeed it must be organic, genetic and dialectical.[7] Such will be Lonergan's own approach as he sets about presenting five main dogmatic theses on the Trinity, but before embarking on that task he sees fit to set forth at length the complex dialectical development from the New Testament to the council of Nicea, hoping thus to provide an adequate context for what follows.

This context-setting, here presented in translation, takes place in ten stages. First there is a discussion of dogmatic development [section I]; then there are separate sections on Jewish Christianity [II], the Gnostics and other sects [III], the Adoptionists, Patripassians and Sabellians [IV], subordinationism [V], "Of one substance" (mainly on Tertullian) [VI], "The image of goodness itself" (mainly on Origen) [VII], the Arians and semi-Arians [VIII] and the *homoousion* [IX]; finally there is an account of the structure of the ante-Nicene movement [X].

In a short preliminary note[8] Lonergan indicates the question that inspires this ten-stage inquiry and guides its progress: how is it that the ancient Christian writers not only did not anticipate the Nicene and subsequent conciliar decrees, but even appear at times to have held the opposite of what was later defined as

[6] *Ibid.*, p. 6.
[7] *Ibid.*, p. 7.
[8] *Ibid.*, p. 15 f.

dogma? With that question answered, he says, the dogmatic theses will become clearer and easier to understand.

Few, I imagine, would find fault with Lonergan's aim, but to some it may seem odd that he begins with a discussion of the nature of dogmatic development, instead of first dealing with Jewish Christianity, the Gnostics, and so on, saving the analysis of dogmatic development for the end.

The same preliminary note provides an explanation. For there Lonergan remarks that just as one must first learn the science of economics before one can apply it to understanding ancient empires and interpreting their history, so one must have a thorough understanding of the nature of dogmatic development before one can discover its elements in the ante-Nicene authors and grasp their intelligible order. In other words, one must know in advance what sort of thing one is looking for, because the texts will only answer questions, they will not speak for themselves, announcing that they are illustrating dogmatic development, telling in detail how they are doing so, and explaining the significance of what they are doing. So with a general understanding of dogmatic development one approaches the historical data and then, at the end of one's inquiry, one can give an account of the structure of a particular development—in this case the one that culminated in Nicea.

With the ground prepared in the manner indicated, Lonergan goes on, in the second part of the first volume, to present five dogmatic theses on (1) the Son's consubstantiality with the Father, (2) the divinity of the Holy Spirit, (3) the trinity of consubstantial persons, distinguished from each other by relations, (4) the procession of the Holy Spirit from the Father and the Son and (5) the Trinity both as a mystery in the proper sense of the word, surpassing human understanding, and also as accessible, though only in imperfect, analogical understanding, to reason illumined by faith. The volume ends with a long (23 pages) *scholion* on the psychological analogy, which, Lonergan is careful to explain, he is here treating neither as positive theologian nor as systematic theologian, but as dogmatic theologian.

The second volume opens with a short *prooemium*,[9] in which Lonergan states the aim and outlines the structure of the work. His concern now, he says, is with that very fruitful, if imperfect understanding of the mysteries that the first Vatican council' asserted to be accessible to reason illumined by faith. Thus the aim is not to present a complete theology of the Trinity, but only that part that is in the strict sense speculative. Taken for granted at this stage are not only the relevant dogmas, but also all the conclusions derived from the sources of revelation: taken for granted is the certitude of faith; the only thing sought now is an understanding of what is already grasped as certain.

A first, long chapter treats of this theological understanding both in itself and in its relationship to the rest of theology. Succeeding chapters seek to induce in readers the desired understanding of the divine processions, the real divine relations, the divine persons considered in themselves, the divine persons compared with each other, and the divine missions. While metaphysical and psychological considerations contribute greatly to theological understanding, fuller treatment of some important questions is consigned to appendices, only the minimum necessary being included in the main presentation.[10] Finally, those who wish to delve more deeply into the historical or the speculative question are referred to the *Verbum* articles and to *Insight*, respectively.

II

Lonergan first taught a course on the Trinity at the College of the Immaculate Conception in Montreal, during the academic year, 1945-46. The preparation and teaching of this course must have coincided with the preparation for publication of the series of articles entitled "The concept of *verbum* in the writings of St.

[9] *De Deo Trino*, II, p. 5.

[10] There are three appendices, the first on the notion of immanent operation, the second on the act of understanding, the third on relations; together these appendices cover 55 pages.

Thomas Aquinas", the first of which appeared in the September, 1946, issue of *Theological Studies*.[11] In a full-scale study of Lonergan's work the *Verbum* articles would have to be treated at considerable length,[12] but here a few brief comments must suffice.

First, as a work of interpretation these articles are a fruit of what Lonergan has called his "years reaching up to the mind of Aquinas",[13] and one may add that the results of his investigation ran counter to a solidly established view of what Aquinas meant, thus challenging the authenticity of a long tradition of interpretation.

Secondly, the articles raised questions of the greatest significance for philosophy, especially for cognitional theory; for the crux of the matter is the function of the act of insight (understanding, *intelligere*) within human cognitional process, and Lonergan was convinced that a centuries-long neglect of insight had not only blocked access to Aquinas' meaning, but also greatly impoverished both theology and philosophy.[14]

---

[11] The second and third articles appeared in the same journal in March and September, 1947, the fourth and fifth in March and September, 1949. The whole series was published as *Verbum, Word and Idea in Aquinas*, Edited by David B. Burrell, C.S.C., with an introduction by Lonergan himself, London, Darton, Longman & Todd, Ltd., 1968. My page-references will be to this edition, but the numbering is the same in the American edition, University of Notre Dame Press, 1967.

[12] See David Tracy. *The Achievement of Bernard Lonergan*. New York, Herder and Herder, 1970, chapter three: "The *Verbum* articles: The Recovery of the World of Thomist Interiority", and references there, p. 54, n. 6.

[13] *Insight. A Study of Human Understanding*. London, Longmans, Green & Co., now published by Darton, Longman & Todd, Ltd., and New York, Philosophical Library, 1957, p. 748.

[14] A central question in the historical inquiry is about the data on which Aquinas focussed attention in his effort to understand *verbum*. For Lonergan the answer is that he focussed attention on the data of his own rational consciousness—the language he uses may be metaphysical, but the meaning expressed is derived from subtle self-attention. Interpreters can fail to grasp the fact that if they are to understand correctly Aquinas' thought on *verbum*, they must pay attention to the operations of their own minds.

Thirdly, although they raise wider issues, the primary concern of the *Verbum* articles is with the specifically trinitarian question of identifying precisely and working out accurately the human analogy to intelligible emanations in God. It is not only, as Lonergan remarks, that "St. Thomas' thought on *verbum* occurs, for the most part, in a trinitarian context",[15] but also that what inspired him to undertake the investigation in the first place was the current state of trinitarian theology. In his brief introduction to the final article, which, under the general title of the series, bears the particular title, *Imago Dei*, he remarks (echoing the introduction to the whole series) that "in prevalent theological opinion there is as good an analogy to the procession of the Word in human imagination as in human intellect, while the analogy to the procession of the Holy Spirit is wrapped in the deepest obscurity".[16] He then continues:

> "It seemed possible to eliminate the obscurity connected with the second procession by eliminating the superficiality connected with opinions on the first. With this end in view we have devoted four articles to an exploration of related points in Thomist metaphysics and rational psychology. We now turn to the *imago Dei*, which is the central issue both in Aquinas' thought on *verbum* and, as well, in our inquiry".[17]

The fruit of the investigation of *verbum* continues to appear in all of Lonergan's later work on the Trinity.

Lonergan next taught a course on the Trinity during the academic year, 1949–50, at Regis College (then the College of Christ the King), Toronto. The last of the *Verbum* articles had just appeared, in the September, 1949, issue of *Theological Studies*, and *Insight* was already in process of composition, but during this year Lonergan also found time to produce a substantial set of Latin notes (amounting to perhaps 30,000 words)

A very helpful entry into this problem is provided by Lonergan himself in his introduction to the Burrell edition of *Verbum*, pp. vii–xv.

[15] *Verbum*, p. xiv.
[16] *Ibid.*, p. 183.
[17] *Ibid.*

on the knowledge and will of God,[18] to go not with his course on the Trinity, but with a course entitled *De Deo Uno*, of which he gave a part.

In 1953 came the move to Rome, where Lonergan was to spend twelve years as Professor of Theology at the Gregorian University. There he had a steady commitment to courses on the Trinity and the Incarnation, offered in alternate years, the course on the Trinity occurring five times in all, the first time during the year 1954-55, the last during the year 1962-63.[19] There is a set of notes entitled *De Sanctissima Trinitate*, dated 7 March, 1955, which belongs to the first of these courses. Called a supplement, obviously because it was intended to supplement the standard textbook named for the course, this set of notes is also an early step in the preparation of Lonergan's first textbook on the Trinity, and so it provides the transition to our next topic.[20]

III

To begin from the final product, we recall that the twin-volume *De Deo Trino*, with its separate dogmatic and systematic parts, was published in 1964. In describing the earlier stages of development it will be best to start with the systematic part,

[18] *De scientia atque voluntate Dei*. Toronto, College of Christ the King, 1950 (typescript). The best available editions of this and of several other unpublished early Latin works of Lonergan are those prepared under the general editorship of Frederick E. Crowe, S.J., who, as well as providing separate introductions, has provided a very helpful general introduction. The "Regis Edition" is available for study at The Lonergan Centre, Regis College, Toronto, and at the Lonergan Centres of Milltown Park, Dublin, and of Canisius College, Sydney, Australia.

[19] These courses were for very large undergraduate classes, of more than 600 students. There was also a course for doctoral students, *On the divine Persons*, in 1955-56.

[20] These notes contain three articles: (1) Certain general notions, (2) The image of God in man, (3) From the image to the eternal exemplar; the first two articles were reprinted with very slight changes as appendices I and II in *Divinarum personarum* . . .; see next note, and cf. note 10, above.

because it is a third, revised edition of Lonergan's first textbook on the Trinity, entitled (I translate) *The analogical conception of the divine persons*.[21] In his preface to the 1964 edition Lonergan relates this work to a particular stage in his own development. He tells us that in his effort to distinguish and relate the various parts of theology the first thing he learned was how different from those of all the other parts were the aim, the proper object and the method of systematic theology, and it was as a sample, or illustration, of systematic theology that he produced *The analogical conception . . .*[22] A second edition of the work appeared in 1959, unchanged, except for correction of misprints and two minor additions; but the third and final edition, which became *De Deo Trino, II: Pars systematica*, contains some considerable revision, not least in the opening chapter, where Lonergan introduces some new reflections on the nature of systematic theology.

In 1961 there appeared *De Deo Trino: Pars analytica*.[23] This work Lonergan relates to a second stage in his development.[24] He tells us that, having distinguished systematic theology from the other branches of theology, he next grasped how different were the aim, the proper object and the method of dogmatic theology from those of positive theology in the strict sense, and it was as a sample, or illustration, of dogmatic theology that he produced the "Analytic part". This he revised for the 1964 edition, and he substituted "Dogmatic Part" for "Analytic part" in the title.[25]

[21] *Divinarum personarum conceptio analogica.* Gregorian University, Rome, 1957, p. 302 (ad usum auditorum). The phrase in parentheses, "for the use of students", indicates that Lonergan did not intend the work for publication in the full sense of the word. The phrase appears also on his *De constitutione Christi ontologica et psychologica*, Gregorian University, Rome, 1956, 1958[2], 1961[3], 1964[4], and on his *De Verbo Incarnato*, Gregorian University, Rome, 1960, 1961[2], and (revised) 1964[3].

[22] *De Deo Trino*, I, p. 3.

[23] Gregorian University, Rome, 1961, p. 326. Again, technically "for the use of students".

[24] *De Deo Trino*, I, *loc. cit.*

[25] In drawing attention (*ibid.*, p. 4) to the main differences between the

IV

Even from the above brief account it is clear how intertwined is Lonergan's trinitarian theology with his thought on theological method. His deep interest in method goes back at least as far as the late 1930's, when he was working in Rome on his doctoral dissertation on St. Thomas' thought on operative grace, which begins with a long theoretical discussion of speculative development.[26] Writing in 1964 on this first major work of Lonergan's, F. E. Crowe expressed the view that for all the wealth of ideas it contained, ideas that continued to fertilise Lonergan's thought in various areas during the following decades, "the real value of the dissertation did not lie in points of objective doctrine at all, but in factors that are more subjective and methodological, factors that for this reason are far more fundamental; in this respect the influence of Lonergan's initial work on his subsequent development can hardly be exaggerated".[27]

The interest in method appears again in the early (unpublished) Latin writings. For example, a set of class-notes (1946) on the

---

revised and the first edition of this part, Lonergan notes in the first place pages 3–28; these pages include: (1) the preface itself, (2) the introduction, which I discussed on p. x f. above, and (3) the section on dogmatic development, which is the first section of the present translation.

Incidentally, the phrase "for the use of students" does not appear on the 1964 edition of *De Deo Trino*.

[26] Four articles based on this study appeared under the title, "St. Thomas' Thought on Gratia Operans", in *Theological Studies*, 2 (1941) 289–324; (1942) 69–88; 375–402; 533–578. These articles were published as *Grace and Freedom*, edited by J. Patout Burns, S.J., London, Darton, Longman & Todd, Ltd., 1971 (also available at Seabury Press, New York). Lonergan did not publish the introductory section to which I have just referred in the text.

[27] *Spirit as Inquiry. Studies in honor of Bernard Lonergan, S.J.* Edited by Frederick E. Crowe, S.J. *Continuum*, 2 (1964), p. 18.

supernatural order[28] contains in its introduction a brief discussion of the twofold order of ideas, the first (here called "resolutory") proceeding from revealed truths to their intelligible ordering, the second (here called "compository") descending from the intelligible ordering to the ordered elements. In the treatise itself Lonergan adopts the second order, which he understands as the appropriate order for teaching more advanced students, the first order being the appropriate one for teaching beginners. This is the start of a long-lasting exploration of what Lonergan came to call the analytic and the synthetic order of human thinking. By 1950[29] they have become the way of discovery ("via inventionis") and the way of teaching ("via doctrinae"), and they are two different parts of theology, the first concerned with faith, the second with understanding.

With the *Verbum* articles begins the discussion of method in the context of trinitarian theology. The final section of the final article[30] is headed *"Via Doctrinae"* and in it Lonergan insists that without a grasp of the twofold ordering of our trinitarian concepts we cannot appreciate what St. Thomas is doing in his treatment of the Trinity in the *Summa theologiae*. The significance of St. Thomas' procedure, he says, is that it places his trinitarian theory in a class by itself,[31] and a little later he says: ". . . the *via doctrinae* of the *Summa* is a masterpiece of theology as science and the apex of trinitarian speculation".[32]

---

[28] *De ente supernaturali*. College of the Immaculate Conception, Montreal, 1946. See note 18, above, on the early Latin works.

[29] In the treatise on the knowledge and will of God; see note 18, above. Cf. F. E. Crowe, "Early Jottings on Bernard Lonergan's Method in Theology", *Science et Esprit*, Vol. xxv, January–April, 1973, 121–138; on the present point, p. 124. For further relevant comment, see Crowe's introduction to the Regis edition, p. x f.

The idea of the ways (or orders) of composition/resolution and discovery/teaching is not of course Lonergan's personal creation, but is taken over from Aquinas. See *Verbum*, Index, under *Via*.

[30] *Verbum*, pp. 206–215.

[31] *Ibid.*, p. 206.

[32] *Ibid.*, p. 211.

In an article entitled, "Theology and Understanding", published in 1954[33]—an article mainly concerned with the nature and role of speculative theology—Lonergan treated the twofold order of discovery and teaching more fully than he had done before, and as a concrete instance of the order of teaching he adduced St. Thomas' treatment of the Trinity in the *Summa*. Comparing the arrangement of questions there with what he calls "the magnificent disorder of the *Scriptum super sententias*", "the conspicuous order of the *Contra gentiles*" and "the still different order of the *De potentia*", he remarks, "It would seem that Aquinas had conducted a rather elaborate experiment in theological method", and he goes on to say that while he cannot attempt even an outline of Aquinas' successive essays, "it may be worth while to indicate schematically just how the *ordo inventionis* and the inverse *ordo doctrinae* are related in trinitarian theory".[34] From this time forward trinitarian theology would seem to have been the area in which, mainly, Lonergan worked out his method in theology. In the years from 1954 to 1963 he offered half a dozen courses on method to doctoral students at the Gregorian,[35] and in Summer Institutes in Canada and the United States he expressed his developing ideas on method; in all of this he was, of course, ranging far and wide, outside the field of trinitarian theology, yet it was apparently within that field that he located the questions of method most sharply, and it was there that he gave his most deliberate and elaborate illustrations of method in action.[36]

---

[33] *Gregorianum*, 35 (1954), 630–648. Reprinted in *Collection. Papers by Bernard Lonergan, S.J.* Edited by Frederick E. Crowe, S.J., London, Darton, Longman & Todd, Ltd., and New York, Herder and Herder, 1967, pp. 121–141.

[34] *Collection*, p. 129.

[35] The titles of these courses were (I translate): (1) "A Theoretic Inquiry into Methods in General" (1954–55); (2) "Intellect and Method" (1958–59 and 1960–61); (3) "System and History" (1959–60); (4) "Method in Theology" (1961–62 and 1963–64).

[36] One must not forget, however, that Lonergan was also deeply involved during these years with the closely-related theology of the Incarnation.

V

If trinitarian theology has its importance for Lonergan as the area in which, mainly, he worked out his method in theology, it has of course the greatest importance as itself a question in theology. And if it is acknowledged that Lonergan has made a significant contribution to method, it may still be asked whether he has made any specific contribution to trinitarian theology itself. More radically, one might question the relevance of any trinitarian theology for our complex, crisis-ridden contemporary world, but even allowing (as Christian theologians do) that since God remains relevant, the Father, the Son and the Holy Spirit remain relevant also, one may still ask (as some Christian theologians do) whether the trinitarian and christological doctrines of the early Church councils retain any relevance, or whether there is any point to rather remote and abstruse speculations on the internal relations of the Trinity; and so, turning to Lonergan's trinitarian theology, one might ask whether it has any lasting significance, beyond that of witnessing to a tradition and documenting a personal history.

Such questions are not lightly to be brushed aside, but neither can they be answered briefly and simply, in a manner utterly convincing to those who are unable or unwilling to work through just such works as Lonergan's *De Deo Trino*. On the more basic issue, whether trinitarian theology is relevant at all, one might at least begin by asking in reply how valuable, in the long-run, will a charismatic, or pentecostal movement be, if it is not informed by adequate trinitarian theory; or how important, in the last analysis, is Jesus Christ, if we do not know him to be truly God as well as truly man, and if we are not struggling to advance in understanding of what that means. But then it can be asked, what kind of trinitarian theology is relevant? For some have found Lonergan's trinitarian theology extremely traditional and have suggested that it is largely a kind of theological archaeology. On this I would make a brief, two-part comment.

First, Lonergan yields to no one in his concern for a thoroughly modern, post-classical, methodical theology, but neither does he yield to anyone in his insistence that such an ongoing theology must be grounded in a critical assimilation of past achievement. In *Method in Theology*, having presented his eightfold division of functional specialties, he goes on to assign grounds for the division, the first ground being that theological operations occur in two basic phases:

> "If one is to harken to the word, one must also bear witness to it. If one engages in *lectio divina*, there come to mind *quaestiones*. If one assimilates tradition, one learns that one should pass it on. If one encounters the past, one also has to take one's stand towards the future. In brief, there is a theology *in oratione obliqua* that tells what Paul and John, Augustine and Aquinas, and anyone else had to say about God and the economy of salvation. But there is also a theology *in oratione recta* in which the theologian, enlightened by the past, confronts the problems of his own day".[37]

The concern expressed in this passage for both past and future was powerfully operative in Lonergan himself from his earliest years as scholar and teacher—one need only refer to his own assessment of his Aquinas studies on the one hand, and of *Insight* on the other, as two quite different kinds of contribution to Pope Leo XIII's programme, *vetera novis augere et perficere*, the former aimed at establishing what the *vetera* really were, the latter exploring the possibilities of what the *nova* might be.[38]

Secondly, in his trinitarian theology Lonergan in fact does more than assimilate the past. David Tracy, reflecting on the years in Rome when, having completed *Insight*, Lonergan produced his treatises on the Trinity and the Incarnation, finds him already in possession of a "new critical technique to control meaning", one fruit of which is that it "has made possible

---

[37] *Method in Theology*. London, Darton, Longman & Todd, Ltd., 1972 (also available at Seabury Press, New York), p. 133. The functional specialties of phase one are Research, Interpretation, History and Dialectic; those of phase two are Foundations, Doctrines, Systematics and Communications.

[38] See *Verbum*, p. 220 and *Insight*, p. 747 f.

Lonergan's often startling developments on a number of particular Trinitarian and Christological problems".[39] I do not wish to undertake a fuller discussion of this point, and so I shall simply appeal to the conviction of many contemporary theologians that *De Deo Trino* contains an enormous amount of untapped wealth, that ought to be made more widely available through translation.[40]

VI

Why has Lonergan—at least so far and in spite of frequent urging—released for publication in translation only one sixth of *De Deo Trino*? I do not presume to offer a complete explanation, but at least I can suggest a few reasons. The first reason, in fact, applies equally to all parts of the work and so, for all its strength, it has obviously had less than absolute force. It is simply the fact that the work was originally composed in Latin, and Lonergan is convinced that he was severely inhibited in expression by the inherent limitations of that language (he has, incidentally, an excellent command of Latin), so that a translation would not fairly represent his actual thinking at the time of composition. When I first approached him about a possible translation he spoke of this problem, and I recall such phrases as, "if you have to use Latin, you just do what you can", and, "Latin is fine, if you have nothing to say that Marcus Tullius Cicero could not have said".

The second reason is the major development that took place

---

[39] David Tracy, *op. cit.*, p. 204 f.

[40] Most often mentioned in this context are the later chapters of the systematic part: in chapter four, the discussion of the term "person" as applied to God; in chapter five, the analogy of temporal and eternal subjects, and the Trinity as three distinct subjects of one divine consciousness; in chapter six, the treatment of the divine missions and the explanation of the indwelling of the Trinity. Of the dogmatic part Lonergan was most of all urged to release the part that he has in fact released.

in Lonergan's thinking about method in theology after the publication of *De Deo Trino* in 1964. This reason would apply particularly to the introduction to the first volume and the long first chapter of the second, where Lonergan distinguishes and relates positive, dogmatic and systematic theology. By his own account, it was in February, 1965, that he achieved the breakthrough that brought him from this position to the eight functional specialties of *Method in Theology*.[41] Naturally enough he is now inclined to say that his views on method in theology are to be sought in the book of that name, not in the Latin writings of an earlier period. I am convinced that the methodological sections of *De Deo Trino* contain an abundance of precious and permanently valid insights, and that they do much more than document stages in Lonergan's own development. Still, when talking to Lonergan I made the case for translation of these sections rather less forcefully than I might have done, for fear of seeming to diminish the significance of the recently published *Method in Theology*.

A third reason—not unrelated to the two already mentioned—applies to the thesis-section of the dogmatic part and, to a much lesser extent I should think, to chapters two to six of the systematic part. The problem here is the whole framework within which Lonergan had to teach theology from 1940 to 1965, to which, in lectures, conversations and writings, he has in the past several years made frequent reference. Of the period during which he produced *De Verbo Incarnato* and *De Deo Trino* he says it was one ". . . in which the situation I was in was hopelessly

---

[41] It would be something of a caricature to think of Lonergan having, until February, 1965, only three "things", and then finding himself suddenly with eight "things". Already in 1957 The *Analogical conception*. . . . added to a consideration of the analytic and synthetic movements in theology a consideration of "a third, historical movement" (pages 28–41); and in the introduction to the first part of *De Deo Trino*, as I have already remarked, Lonergan insists that the dogmatic theologian's approach must be concrete, organic, genetic and dialectical. Still, though there are what can now be seen as hints of what was to come, the breakthrough was dramatic.

antiquated, but had not yet been demolished . . ."[42] And else-where, more generally: "I taught theology for twenty-five years under impossible conditions".[43] What he had particularly in mind was that ". . . to be a professor in dogmatic theology was to be a specialist in the Old Testament—not just in the Pentateuch or something like that—the Old Testament, the New, the Apostolic Fathers, the Greek Fathers, the ante-Nicene, Greek and Latin, the post-Nicene, the medieval Scholastics, the Renaissance period, the Reformation, contemporary philosophy and so on".[44]

Now within that system teaching was by the thesis method: the professor stated his thesis, defined the terms he was using, assigned a theological note[45] to the thesis (or perhaps different notes to the different parts of it), gave a survey of "adversaries", ranging at times over two millennia, provided arguments in favour of the thesis from Scripture, from the Fathers, from the Church councils, from the Popes, from the ordinary *magisterium* of the Church, from the theologians, often adding a suasive "theological reason", before, finally, answering objections.

The dogmatic part of *De Deo Trino* remains basically within that framework, which Lonergan would surely not have chosen had he not been writing for classes of more than 600 theological students at the Gregorian University. He would not deny, I am sure, that there is a great deal of wealth in his five dogmatic

[42] "An interview with Fr. Bernard Lonergan, S.J." Edited by Philip McShane, *The Clergy Review* 56 (1971), 412–431. Reprinted in Bernard Lonergan *A Second Collection*. Edited by William F. J. Ryan, S.J., and Bernard Tyrrell, S.J., London, Darton, Longman & Todd, Ltd., and Philadelphia, Westminster Press, 1974, 209–230. The quotation is from p. 213 of this book.

[43] Bernard Lonergan. *Philosophy of God, and Theology*, London, Darton, Longman & Todd, Ltd., and Philadelphia, Westminster Press, 1973, p. 15.

[44] *A Second Collection, loc. cit.* I draw attention to the fact that the printed text of this interview was edited from a tape-recording.

[45] The theological note was rather like a grade on a certainty-scale: the highest grade assignable was "of defined faith"; quite low, but satisfactory, was "more probable"; failing grades were given to the positions of the "adversaries", the lowest grade normally being "heretical".

theses on the Trinity (neither would he deny that there was a
value in the thesis system itself, if used intelligently), but he would
be very aware that the task of extracting that wealth and dis-
playing it in appropriate English dress would be a difficult and
a delicate one, involving much more than straightforward
translation And so, I think, he prefers to leave it where it is for
the present, for those with interest, energy and ability enough to
discover it for themselves. As I have said, I think that this reason
for resisting translation has considerably less force when applied
to the systematic part, principally because there Lonergan is
involved with only one, very specific, theological task—in the
language of *Method in Theology*, a single functional specialty—
whereas in the dogmatic part he ranges over as many as five.[46]

Why, then, if Lonergan was unwilling to release so little, was
he willing to release even so much as he did? Because, I believe,
if the situation in which, as professor of theology, he found
himself, was "hopelessly antiquated", it does not follow that it
crippled him entirely, leaving him incapable of producing work
that would endure. Doing what you could within the system
included, he tells us himself, introducing what you could, and
he illustrates his meaning by referring to the very part of *De
Deo Trino* that is here presented in translation. He says:

"For example, my analysis of the Ante-Nicene period on trinitarian
doctrine: I was developing there also what I consider something permanently valid, namely this type of interpretation that is concerned with things
that the thinkers themselves didn't think about. Tertullian has a Stoic
background, Origen has a middle Platonist background, Athanasius'
account of Nicea is something totally new that you can't reduce to anything

[46] It is a delicate matter to try to transpose from the earlier categories of "way
of discovery","way of teaching", "analytic way","synthetic way", to the
categories of *Method in Theology*, and one had best be tentative. In a footnote
to a still unpublished paper, "Christology Today: Methodological Reflections",
presented at Université Laval, Quebec, in March, 1975, Lonergan remarks that
the *via doctrinae*, in which Aquinas composed his *Summa theologiae*, corresponds
to the functional specialty, Systematics, of *Method in Theology*. He adds: "The
via inventionis would cover the first four or perhaps five previous specialties."
(Ms. p. 33, n. 10.)

Platonic, Aristotelian, Gnostic or Stoic and so on; a new situation is created. It's second-level thinking, the sort of thing that is possible within a Hellenistic culture. But that comparison of all three, revealing their different backgrounds—the different ways in which they conceived the Son to be divine, totally different ways—is an understanding of the process from the New Testament to Nicea. That, I think, is something valid".[47]

Praise from scholars whom he respects strengthened Lonergan's conviction that at least this part of De Deo Trino had enduring value. But for that conviction to be strong enough to break down his general resistance to translation it must, I think, have included the judgment that this study of the ante-Nicene period could, in the post-Method context, be recognised as theology in its first phase (in oratione obliqua), culminating in the functional specialization of Dialectic.[48]

A further reason that may have swayed Lonergan refers directly to the results of his investigation of the ante-Nicene period. We recall that the immediate aim of this particular part of De Deo Trino was to provide a context within which five dogmatic theses on the Trinity would be better understood and, one may add here, not rejected through misunderstanding of their meaning. If Lonergan urges theologians to make a major shift to a methodical theology, capable of responding to the complex challenge of the late twentieth century, he also urges them not to abandon the definitions of Nicea, Constantinople I, Ephesus, Chalcedon and Constantinople III. He has, in fact, been very disturbed by what he considers aberrations in theology, including Catholic theology, on the specific question of the divinity of Christ, and he would say that such aberrations are based to a large extent on a defective understanding of what was actually going forward in the Church from the time of the New Testament to the council of Nicea.[49] For Lonergan, as the reader

[47] A Second Collection, loc. cit.

[48] On Dialectic, as a functional specialty, see Method in Theology, pp. 128-130, and chapter 10, pp. 235-266.

[49] See, for example, A Second Collection, pp. 11-32: "The Dehellenization of Dogma", and pp. 292-305: "The Origins of Christian Realism". The paper, "Christology Today" (see note 46, above), takes up this topic again.

of this translation can easily see, the original emergence of dogma, and of the very notion of dogma, was not an aberration, not a betrayal of the genuine religious spirit of primitive Christianity, not a migration to the cold and barren climate of Greek metaphysics, but a genuine development; if his study of the ante-Nicene movement could help to establish this point, he could not but be pleased. For much as he wants theologians to build for the future, no less does he want their building to arise on firm foundations, and if the council of Nicea did not say the last word in theology, it did say a word that remains true today.

Some readers may be disappointed not to find Lonergan coming to grips with the christological questions raised by contemporary theologians such as Rahner, Pannenberg, Wiles, Schoonenberg and others.[50] May I remind them that what is here presented in translation is only a fraction of what Lonergan has to say on the matter of trinitarian and christological theology, and as he himself says repeatedly, a man cannot do everything at once.

VII

My task of translation has been both rewarding and difficult. There is no translation without interpretation, and often enough I was so fearful of misinterpreting Lonergan that the work came almost to a standstill. One danger of such a fear is that it could lead to a slavish, literal translation, which not only would read very badly, but also might well amount to a more serious misinterpretation. While trying to avoid this danger, I was at the same time wary of translating too freely and thus losing the flavour of the original, and I was particularly aware of the danger that I might make the Lonergan of *De Deo Trino* say what I thought the Lonergan of *Method* would now say. I was tempted

[50] In the paper referred to in the previous note he does in fact deal at some length with Fr. Schoonenberg.

to try at least to soften the impact on the unsympathetic of some rather sharp statements about heresies and heretics (e.g. p. 49), or of the brief comparison of dogmas with Euclidean propositions (pp. 4 f.), by referring in footnotes to later, more extended and more nuanced treatments of the same topics, but I thought it better to trust the reader to recall the time and circumstances of the original composition, rather than badger him by what could so easily appear to be special pleading. My aim has been to provide an accurate and readable translation that also preserves something of the style and tone of the original Latin, and I hope that, in spite of inadequacies, it may have some value.

In the original Latin text there are many quotations from ante-Nicene authors, and I wondered how I should handle them. Eventually, for the sake of some sort of uniformity in English style, I first translated all of these passages myself, risking, and sometimes falling into, the traps that await the non-specialist. I have since checked my versions against published translations, and at times have borrowed phrases and sentences, and I hope that I have thus eliminated at least my most egregious blunders.

Many friends have given me much-needed encouragement, and I thank them all. I must, however, single out Frederick E. Crowe, S. J., of Regis College, Toronto, for special mention—but for his constant encouragement, and his generosity in sharing with me his very special knowledge of Lonergan's work, I could not have brought this project, small enough as it seems, to completion. My sincere thanks also to John C. Kelly, S.J., of Milltown Park, Dublin, who kindly relieved me of the burden of preparing the index. To Bernard Lonergan himself I am of course particularly grateful, for his trust that I would not do him a great disservice, and for more, besides, than I can attempt to calculate. Finally, my thanks to John Todd, of Darton, Longman & Todd, who encouraged the project initially and has been the essence of gentle patience ever since.

ABBREVIATIONS

ACW   *Ancient Christian Writers,* Westminster & London, 1946 ff.

AW   H. G. Opitz, Athanasius Werke,[1] Berlin & Leipzig, 1934.

CSEL   *Corpus scriptorum ecclesiasticorum latinorum,* 1866 ff.

DBS   Pirot-Robert, *Dictionnaire de la Bible, Supplément,* 1928 ff.

DS   Denziger–Schönmetzer, *Enchiridion Symbolorum,* ed. 32, 1963.

DTC   Vacant-Mangenot-Amann, *Dictionnaire de théologie catholique,* 1902 ff.

EP   Rouët de Journal, *Enchiridion patristicum,* ed. 7, 1929.

GCS   *Griechische christliche Schriftsteller,* 1897 ff.[2]

Hahn   A. & L. Hahn, *Bibliothek der Symbole und Glaubensregeln der alten Kirche,* ed. 3, 1897.

HE   Historia ecclesiastica (Eusebius, Socrates, Theodoret).

LTK   Höfer-Rahner, *Lexikon für Theologie und Kirche,* 1957 ff.

MG   J. Migne, *Patrologia graeca,* 1857 ff.

ML   J. Migne, *Patrologia latina,* 1844 ff.

SC   *Sources chrétiennes,* 1941 ff.

---

[1] See the reservations expressed by J. Lebon, *Rev. hist. eccl.,* 31 (1935), 161 f., 627 f.

[2] It is customary to refer to the various editors: Baehrens, Holl, Klostermann, Koetschau, Preuschen, Stählin, Wendland, Whittaker. . . .

SECTION I

DOGMATIC DEVELOPMENT

Dogmatic development, viewed in its totality, has four main aspects: an objective, a subjective, an evaluative and a hermeneutical aspect.[1]

The objective aspect appears from a comparison of the gospels with conciliar documents. The gospels, and the apostolic writings generally, are not just a collection of true propositions, addressed only to the mind of the reader; they teach the truth, but in such a way that they penetrate the sensibility, fire the imagination, engage the affections, touch the heart, open the eyes, attract and impel the will of the reader. Conciliar decrees are totally different: so clearly and so accurately do they declare what is true that they seem to bypass the senses, the feelings and the will, to appeal only to the mind. More seriously, it might be argued, the councils do not faithfully reproduce in scriptural language the many truths propounded in the scriptures; between the scriptures and the councils there intervenes a process of synthesis, by which many sayings of scripture are reduced to a single, fundamental proposition, frequently expressed in technical terms.

In its objective aspect, then, dogmatic development contains two distinct elements, which are also two kinds of transition. The first of these transitions is from one literary genre to another: the scriptures are addressed to the whole person, whereas the

[1] We presume familiarity with the theological treatises on God's special providence, divine revelation, the inspiration of sacred scripture and the *magisterium* of the Church.

councils aim only at enlightening the intellect. The second transition pertains to the order of truth: where scripture presents a multitude of truths, a conciliar pronouncement expresses one single truth, which is related to the many truths of scripture as a kind of principle or foundation.

To this objective aspect of dogmatic development there corresponds of necessity a subjective aspect. For if there is a change in literary genre and a change in the manner of apprehending and considering the truth, then there is a change in man himself. But what exactly is this change in man himself?[2]

To begin with what is most obvious, there is no doubt that the interior state of a person who is asleep and dreaming is quite different from that of one who is wide awake: the kind of law that governs the succession and interrelation of dream-images, and the kind of pattern in which they emerge, are totally different from the patterns and laws that govern and order our daytime experiences. Not so obvious, perhaps, is the fact that waking consciousness is anything but a uniform, homogeneous state— that there are many different patterns in which our conscious acts emerge, some preceding and calling forth others, others following and complementing those that preceded them and called them forth. Quite different from each other are the interior states that accompany involvement with practical problems, the enjoyment of aesthetic experience, the arousal of mythic consciousness, the ardour of mystical illumination, the joyful sharing of friends in human intersubjectivity, and the specifically intellectual pursuits of the scientific mind.

Conscious human acts emerge, therefore, within different patterns of experience, patterns that can be identified and described, distinguished from and related to each other. But the basic distinction to be made is between undifferentiated and differentiated consciousness. Consciousness is undifferentiated where the whole person is involved, operating simultaneously

[2] For a fuller treatment of the topic see Bernard Lonergan, *Insight. A Study of Human Understanding*, London, Longmans, Green and Co., and New York, Philosophical Library, 1957, chapter VI, 2; pp. 181 ff.

and equally with all of his powers. Differentiated consciousness, on the other hand, is capable of operating exclusively, or at least principally, on a single level, while the other levels are either entirely subordinated to the attainment of the goal of that level, or at least are held in check, so that they do not hinder its attainment. In the man of action, for example, imagination, affectivity, will, senses and practical intelligence all operate together: imagination represents the goal to be achieved, affectivity is drawn towards it, will embraces it, practical intelligence, with the aid of the senses, figures out how the goal is to be achieved and how the obstacles are to be removed that stand in the way of its attainment. Thus the whole person, with all his powers, tends towards a goal that is proportionate to man. In contrast, the scientist, or the speculative thinker, tends towards a goal that is not that of the whole man, but only of his intellect. The will is therefore restricted to willing the good of intellect, which is the truth; imagination throws up only those images that induce understanding or suggest a judgment; feelings and emotions, finally, are as if anaesthetised, so firmly are they kept in control.

Bearing this basic distinction in mind, it is not hard to see that what corresponds to the gospels is undifferentiated consciousness, whereas what corresponds to dogma is differentiated consciousness. For the gospels are addressed to the whole person, on all levels of operation. The dogmas, on the contrary, demand a subject who can focus attention on the aspect of truth alone, so that other powers are under the sway of intellect, or else are somehow stilled.

Dogmatic development, therefore, not only presents an objective aspect, which is grasped by comparing earlier with later documents; it also demands a certain subjective change, involving a transition from undifferentiated common sense, which is what is most widespread and most familiar, to the intellectual pattern of experience. And this transition does not occur spontaneously; it comes about only through a slow learning process, sustained by serious effort.

There is, thirdly, the evaluative aspect of dogmatic develop-ment. For it is characteristic of man that he not only acts, but also pauses to reflect on his actions and to pass judgment on them. Admittedly, what can and ought to be done in this regard at later stages of individual or cultural development, is not to be expected at earlier stages, and the criteria by which one judges the self-reflective, self-critical performance of people will vary accordingly. However, we must repeat that dogmatic develop-ment is not something that takes place in a purely objective manner; it also requires human subjects who are sufficiently advanced to be at home in a new, more austere literary genre and to grasp and reflect on the divinely revealed truths in a new manner. If this development of the subject is lacking, or held in little esteem, or left out of account, then it is small wonder that one should wish to bypass dogmas as being rather obscure, or find fault with them as having little religious significance, or even brand them as aberrations. Later, in presenting our theses, we shall have to treat of the truth of dogmas; it will suffice, therefore, if we now consider very briefly whether dogmas are in fact so very obscure and so lacking in religious feeling as many today make them out to be.

It is argued that the dogmas are obscure, whereas the gospels are perfectly clear. In one sense this is true, but in another it is not. It can hardly be said that exegetes find the gospels perfectly clear: today, after almost twenty centuries, the learned articles, the monographs, the commentaries and the dictionaries, the various opinions and hypotheses, the methods and the schools of interpretation would seem to be increasing, not diminishing, in number. And if the gospels are not without obscurity, neither are the dogmas entirely lacking in clarity. Just as Euclid's *Elements* seem very obscure to those who have never learnt geometry, so dogmas, to the uneducated, seem very strange indeed. Yet to mathematicians the meaning of Euclid's *Elements* is so clear and precise that they present almost no problems of interpretation and therefore little ground for disputes among commentators or the never-ending labour of exegetes. And as

4

the mathematician views Euclid, so the theologian views the dogmas of the Church.

The explanation is not hard to find. For when one's other powers are subordinated to one's intellect, one is apt to achieve that clarity and precision that is proper to intellect; those who have made some progress in the intellectual life, therefore, and can move with ease into the intellectual pattern of experience, find nothing more clear and precise than the meaning of a geometrical theorem or of a dogmatic definition. On the other hand, when intellect operates as just one among many diverse powers—and this applies to most people most of the time—then less attention is focussed on the proper end of intellect. In ordinary every-day living there is much that is taken for granted as being sufficiently clear; what is thus taken for granted may be described and stated in detail, from many different angles, but it is normally so tied to particular circumstances, so embedded in the intentions of individual people, that it can never be reduced to the clarity of a definition or a theorem.

So much for the clarity or obscurity of dogmas. We may move on to consider the second contention, that dogmas have little religious significance. This contention is normally coupled with such a glorification of the Hebrew mind, in its ancient simplicity, as to suggest that it was some special gift of God to the Hebrews, sealed with the approval of the scriptures and offered to all future ages as a model to be imitated.

However, the fact is that the farther back we go towards ancient times, the less differentiated we find the consciousness of all men; the esteemed simplicity of the Hebrews, then, is characteristic not of them alone, but of all the more ancient races. Further, the less differentiated one's consciousness and the fewer the patterns of experience in which one lives out one's life, the less clearly, proportionately, does one grasp the diversity of human actions and the less capable, consequently, is one of drawing distinctions between one sphere of action and another. That is why among primitives the spheres of the sacred and the profane interpenetrate, without benefit of distinction or separation,[3] and so those who in secular matters are most religious, in the sphere of religion are most prone to idolatry. The Hebrews themselves were no less inclined to idolatry than were other races; the difference was that their tendency to idolatry was held in check by the inspired teaching of the prophets, proclaimed with vehemence and constantly reiterated. There is little basis, then, for the romantic notion that undifferentiated consciousness is the religious consciousness *par excellence*.

There is no firmer footing for the correlative assertion that dogmas have little religious significance. For it is the function of religion to orientate and direct the whole of man's living towards God, and therefore, as consciousness develops, so too must religion. The simpler one's life-style, the simpler one's religion will be; but when human living becomes highly diversified and highly specialised, then to its many various aspects there correspond many and various functions of religion.

It is plain, therefore, that dogmas pertain to religion most of all because they render differentiated consciousness religious—whether we think of such consciousness as already developed intellectually, or as standing in need of intellectual development. For differentiated consciousness reflects on, and passes judgment on religious matters, as it does on everything else, and such judgments affect the whole tenor and direction of life. And so if one argues that there is nothing religious about intellect, one

[3] The meaning of this interpenetration of the sacred and the profane emerges more clearly when we reflect that the symbolic mentality does not apprehend things as separate and self-contained, as "nothing but . . .", but rather as containing always some further meaning and as revealing and communicating a transcendent reality. Questions about the origin of all things, about God, about the meaning of human life—questions that are raised and answered explicitly by the educated—are handled quite differently by the uneducated, by primitives and by children, who, without benefit of any special conceptual apparatus, raise such questions only by wondering and answer them only by understanding. Cf. W. Wordsworth, *Ode on Intimations of Immortality from Recollections of Early Childhood*. M. Eliade, *Forgerons et Alchimistes*, Paris, 1956, p. 146. M.-J. Congar, art. Théologie, DTC 29 (1946), 386–388, where it is suggested that the Augustinian school of the Middle Ages came out of a symbolic rather than a scientific apprehension of the world.

is not serving the cause of true religion, but rather that of secularism.

But one may say, surely primitives and children can be genuinely religious, and just as surely, religious living does not consist in intellectual exercises. Quite true, but the argument simply misses the point. For religion is not some eternal and immutable Platonic form, with but a single mode of participation for children and adults, for primitives and highly-developed peoples alike. As consciousness develops so too does religion, and so it is fallacious to infer that what is appropriate for children and for primitives constitutes the very essence of religion, always and everywhere the same. Secondly, as we have already said, with the development of consciousness religion takes on many aspects and fulfils many functions; if one particular aspect and function does not constitute the whole of religion, it does not follow that that particular aspect and function is therefore to be denied.

So far we have considered three different aspects of dogmatic development, its objective, its subjective and its evaluative aspect. Now we must move on to the fourth, which is the hermeneutical aspect. This fourth aspect arises because, inevitably, the views one holds about dogmatic development will influence one's investigation and interpretation of that development. The old axiom still remains true, that whatever is received, is received after the manner of the receiver. For the human mind is not equally open to all ideas, like some public square where all may come and go as they please. On the contrary, it is itself a unity, it has an exigence for unity, and it imposes unity on its contents—so much so that every apprehension of data involves, quite naturally and spontaneously, a kind of selection, and every selection, in turn, includes an initial structuring, and every structuring prepares and, in a certain sense, anticipates future judgments. Consequently, not only are there apt to be, as the saying goes, as many opinions on a given topic as there are people holding opinions, but also, when basic issues are at stake, correct apprehension must wait on a kind of conversion.

THE WAY TO NICEA

One finds serious disagreements among historians of dogma, but the sources of these disagreements were already present and operative within the original process of dogmatic development. If one has a false cognitional theory, a false epistemology, or a false metaphysics, one will have little or no understanding of defined dogmas (not without reason are philosophical studies placed before the study of theology); but the same errors and the same tendencies, more or less, which now render dogmas unintelligible or unacceptable, were at work implicitly before the dogmas emerged in the first place, exerting a covert influence against their emergence.

Dogma emerges from the revealed word of God, carried forward by the tradition of the Church; it does so, however, only to the extent that, prescinding from all other riches contained in that word of God, one concentrates on it precisely *as true*. The Judaeo-Christians failed to take this first, small step towards dogma; their practice, rather, was to illustrate the doctrine of the New Testament by images taken from the Old Testament and from the apocalyptic literature.

Secondly, if one separates the word from the truth, if one rejects propositional truth in favour of some other kind of truth, then one is not attending to the word of God as true. Thus, some early Gnostics thought of truth as a kind of wondrous emanation within the divine Pleroma and some moderns think that truth is a matter of things emerging from concealment to reveal themselves to us.

Thirdly, the Adoptionists, who held that the Son of God the Father was a mere man, the Sabellians, who held that he was the very same person as the Father, and the Arians, who held that, though he was at the peak of creation, he was nonetheless a part of creation, all put pressure on the Church to focus attention on the word of God as true. For at the root of these heresies lay the fact that their proponents paid insufficient attention to this particular aspect of God's word.

Fourthly, it is not enough to attend to the word of God as true, if one has a false conception of the relationship between truth and reality. Reality is known through true judgment; explicit knowledge of this fact, however, is a difficult attainment, and it is proportionately rare. There are many who cannot escape from the myth, based on the dominant model of sense-perception, that between truth and reality there intervenes some sort of intellectual vision, perception, or intuition.[4] Such a one was Tertullian: he affirmed that the Son is of one substance with the Father, but this he understood in a kind of organic and more or less materialistic manner.

Fifthly, one does not automatically overcome this error by ascending to the realm of pure spirit. The Platonic ideas, or forms, pertain to a purely spiritual realm, yet they correspond to concepts, not to true judgments. Origen did not quite grasp this point, and so he was led to say that while the Son is the perfect image of the Father, nevertheless he does not possess the divinity itself, but has it only by participation.

What in fact corresponds to the word as true is that which is. And if what is said of the Father is also to be said of the Son, except that the Son is Son, and not Father, it follows that the Son is the same, but not the same person as the Father. And that is the meaning of the term, consubstantial, as used by the council of Nicea. It is also what is meant by the Latin liturgy's preface of the Blessed Trinity: "What from your revelation we believe about your glory, that without difference or distinction we hold about your Son and about the Holy Spirit".

If it was the word of God, considered precisely as true, that led from the gospels to the dogmas, it was the same word, from the same point of view, that brought about what we have described as differentiation of consciousness. For although there are many different states and patterns of consciousness (and it would take volumes to give a tolerably adequate description of any one

---

[4] For a fuller explanation of this point, see our "Metaphysics as Horizon", *Gregorianum*, 44 (1963), 307–318. [This article was reprinted, in *Collection Papers by Bernard Lonergan, S.J.* Edited by F. E. Crowe, S.J., London, Darton, Longman & Todd, Ltd., and New York, Herder and Herder, 1967, pp. 202–220. *Trans.*]

of them), each with its own validity and its own proper place, still, for all their diversity, they are not unconnected; there is a bond that unites them all, so that the same subject can remain in the same world, although he shifts from one pattern of consciousness to another.[5] That bond is the word as true. And that is what we read of in the Sermon on the Mount: "But let your word be 'Yes, Yes' and 'No, No'". Again, it is what we find in dogmatic pronouncements: "If anyone says . . . . let him be anathema". For whenever anyone, whether educated or uneducated, affirms that X is so, he is appropriating the word as true; and similarly, every negation is a rejection of the word as false. Furthermore, no change from one pattern of consciousness to another can make what is true false, or what is false, true. Admittedly, different patterns of consciousness are bounded by different horizons; each has its own particular mode of feeling, thinking and speaking; within different patterns, therefore, there will be different expressions of the same truth. But just as the transition from one pattern of experience, or consciousness, to another, does not destroy the identity of the human subject, neither does it destroy the identity of the truth that he expresses, now within one pattern and now within another.

There is, then, one simple rule for dealing with the arguments adduced by those who say that there is a radical discontinuity between the gospels and the dogmas: pay attention to the word as true. This is what the perceptionists overlook, who think that they know before they have made a judgment. It also escapes the idealists, who insist that what the perceptionists perceive is only the appearance of things, not things in themselves. The essentialists also miss the point, for they can no more distinguish between essence and being, in an adequate manner, than they can between thinking and knowing. There is the same basic flaw in those elaborate descriptions of forms or structures of thought that betray a lack of clear distinction between thinking and knowing. Finally, it is this same failure to attend to the word as true

[5] There are, however, certain states of consciousness in which this bond is no longer present, as in the dream-state, or in madness.

that mars the thinking of those who reduce the dogmas to hellenism; for hellenistic speculation was concerned with essences, whereas dogmas are affirmations of what *is*.[6]

We have enumerated and described four different aspects of dogmatic development: its objective, its subjective, its evaluative and its hermeneutical aspect. Next, we must briefly indicate how closely related these four aspects are to each other; then we shall consider some of their implications.

To begin with, the objective and the subjective aspects are obviously very closely connected, since each is correlative to the other. This is true, of course, in the general sense that every object implies a subject, and every subject a corresponding object, but we mean more than that. Specifically, we mean that the objective aspect of dogmatic development consists in the kind of consideration of the *truth* of what is affirmed that can prescind from all the other components or features of interpersonal communication, and that this presupposes an intellectually developed subject.

Secondly, the evaluative aspect of dogmatic development is intimately connected with its objective and subjective aspects. For, as we have already remarked, it is characteristic of man that he not only acts, but also reflects on his actions, and passes favourable or unfavourable judgments on them. But if different people have different standards of judgment, so that some praise and approve what others blame and disapprove; and if, going beyond mere expressions of praise and blame, of approval and

[6] Theologians in general agree that dogmas affirm the existence of mysteries, whereas theological systems seek some understanding of essences. For example, to say that something *is* or *is not*, *is the same thing* or *is a different thing*, *is in one respect the same and in another different*, is not yet to inquire into essence. Yet such affirmations and distinctions are sufficient to declare the content of the ancient trinitarian and christological dogmas. This point would appear to have escaped J. Hessen (*Griechische oder biblische Theologie?* München/Basel 1962, pp. 86 ff.), perhaps because he acknowledges only the very familiar, commonsense mode of knowing existence. For on the supposition that existence is known only in this way it would follow that one who is in the intellectual pattern of experience can only be speculating about essences.

disapproval, each side attempts by argument to establish its own position and to undermine that of its opponents, then the debate can quickly lead to absolutely fundamental questions. In the original movement towards dogmatic definition these questions were broached only implicitly, the explicit question being, what was to be defined. On the other hand, in the retrospective consideration of defined dogma the same fundamental questions are apt to be clearly stated and explicitly debated.

Thirdly, the hermeneutical and evaluative aspects are intimately related to each other. To repeat the old axiom, whatever is received, is received after the manner of the receiver. Or in other words, whatever is presented to us for our consideration, for approval or disapproval, acceptance or rejection, is received within the horizon constituted by our basic assumptions and convictions. The wide variety of horizons is revealed in questions and disputes about the nature and the validity of dogma—not so much, therefore, in the actual historical investigation of the dogmas, and the manner of interpreting them, as in the judgments passed on their relevance and significance.

Finally, to round off this part of our discussion, we may note that the process of interpretation is twofold, and the art of interpretation has a twofold use. Modern scholarship investigates a long-completed development of dogma, but this retrospective movement of investigation presupposes the earlier, forward movement, beginning with the revealed word of God and ending with dogmatic definition. If the original process of interpretation was direct rather than reflective, in the sense that those involved in it had no sharply-defined awareness of where it was heading; if it seems to have been guided by the chances of history, rather than controlled by scientific method; still, these obvious differences between the two processes must not be allowed to disguise the fact that both come up against the same ultimate questions, that for both the fundamental difficulties are the same. For in each of these two processes, sooner or later one is forced to ask, What is truth? and, What is the relationship between truth and reality?

What follows, then, from all that we have said so far?

In the first place, within the ante-Nicene movement we have to recognise two distinct, though related, developments. There is no doubt that those early Christian centuries produced a development in trinitarian and christological doctrine, but this doctrinal development contained within it another, more profound development: the development of the very notion of dogma. But this latter development was implicit not explicit; the question was not sharply defined, methodically investigated and unambiguously answered. Yet somehow the question was both asked and answered within the process of development which, if it had not taken place, we could not now describe. Investigating that process now from our perspective, we can identify and isolate both the question and the answer in a way that the ante-Nicene authors themselves neither did nor could have done. For those early Christian writers, sometimes directly, sometimes indirectly, paved the way for the definition of dogma, without really knowing what they were doing. This is hardly surprising, since it is a feature of every significant advance in the field of intellect that it must first be accomplished before it can be reflected on, examined in detail, and accurately explained.

Secondly, there is an important distinction to be made between the type of doctrinal development that leads from obscurity to clarity, and the quite different type that leads from one kind of clarity to another. The emergence of the very notion of dogma, grounded in the word of God as true, was a movement from obscurity to clarity; on the other hand, the doctrine of the Christian Church concerning Jesus Christ advanced not from obscurity to clarity, but from one kind of clarity to another. What Mark, Paul and John thought about Christ was neither confused nor obscure, but quite clear and distinct; yet their teaching acquired a new kind of clarity and distinctness through the definition of Nicea. But further dogmas had to follow, and then the historical investigation of dogmas, before the fact and the nature of dogmatic development itself could be clearly established.[7]

[7] For this reason the question of dogmatic development is a much more

Thirdly, we can now see how we have to go about investigating the ante-Nicene development. For we have to deal not with one, but with two distinct developments, and not with two developments of the same type, since one is from obscurity to clarity, the other from one kind of clarity to another. Yet these are not two entirely separate developments, each quite independent of the other, since one is in fact contained in the other, as the generic is contained in the specific—the development of a specific dogma containing within it the development of the notion of dogma itself. Consequently, while every ante-Nicene document is relevant, as long as its subject-matter is the Son of God, our Lord, Jesus Christ, not all are equally relevant. What is most important for our present purpose is a selection of documents that will reveal how differently different authors understood the same thing. For throughout the whole period under discussion it was the same christological doctrine that was handed on; what was developing was the manner in which that doctrine was received; and through that development the notion of dogma emerged from obscurity to clarity, while the knowledge of Jesus Christ advanced from one kind of clarity to another.[8]

---

recent one. Athanasius neither wanted nor intended to bring about dogmatic development; on the contrary, in his profession of faith he would have preferred to use only the words of scripture, if "the malice of the Arians" had not rendered necessary another mode of speech. Cf. *De decretis nicaenae synodi*, 32; AW II, 28, 1 ff.; MG 25, 473D–476A.

[8] It may be helpful to introduce here a comparison with secular studies. It is one thing to ask about the origin of modern science itself, and another to ask about the origin of this or that particular theory or law that is accepted within modern science. The latter task has been undertaken by a very large number of authors writing on very specific topics; the former task was undertaken by Herbert Butterfield, *The Origins of Modern Science, 1300–1800*, London, Bell, 1951, New York, Macmillan Paperbacks, 1960. Butterfield's conclusion shows just how different from each other the two tasks are. For the particular studies show that many diverse components of modern science had been discovered as early as the beginning of the 14th century, but it is Professor Butterfield's contention that modern science itself did not begin until towards the end of the

Fourthly, the two different types of development demand two different methods of inquiry. For while we do indeed ask how much the ante-Nicene authors knew about Christ our Lord, we do not ask how much they knew about dogmatic development (they knew almost nothing about it) but rather what they did to bring it about; and it is clearly one thing to ask what they actually knew and quite another to ask what in fact they did, without knowing what it was that they were doing. If we want to discover how much they knew, then nothing can be admitted as evidence except what they actually said, or at least thought. To apply the same method of inquiry to the task of discovering what they did, unknown to themselves, would inevitably lead to the false conclusion that the ante-Nicene Christian authors did nothing to pave the way for dogma, since they had little or no idea that they were doing anything like that at all.

However, one can acknowledge the need for two different methods of inquiry and still be puzzled about how to go about investigating what people did unknown to themselves. We cannot enter here on a discussion of the variety and distinction of methods, and the grounds for their variety and distinction.

17th century. For the earlier elements remained enclosed within the context established by the Aristotelian system; diverse elements lacked mutual consistency, objections could not be satisfactorily met, and points were readily conceded that modern science would contradict.

The comparison with the question of method is not hard to make. For it is one thing to ask in particular about individual ante-Nicene authors, what each one of them thought about Christ; it is quite another thing to ask about that general movement called dogmatic development, that is illustrated both by the ante-Nicene authors and by others as well. Professor Butterfield could not begin his work until after the completion of a very large number of strictly positive studies of particular questions, and he could not answer his own question before having grasped the significance of system for the proper conception of individual laws. In a somewhat similar manner our present question presupposes a large number of particular positive studies, and even then it cannot be answered without a clear and precise conception of the different aspects of dogmatic development.

Suffice it to say, therefore, that no one is equipped to study dogmatic development whose understanding of dogma and of
development is little better than that of the ante-Nicene authors
themselves. It is not to them that we must look for a precise
understanding either of dogma or of development; neither can
they tell us how many kinds of dogmatic development there are,
or what, in general, one can say about them. On the contrary, it
is the answers to such general questions that provide us with a
certain heuristic structure, in virtue of which, when we come to
study the ante-Nicene authors, we know what to look for, how
to assess and judge what we have found, how to pick out what
is significant, and how to order all the relevant elements in a way
that sets forth the development that they, though unknown to
themselves, in fact brought about. The topic of heuristic structure[9] is, however, a large one, about which we need say no
more at present; it will be enough, for our present purposes, if
the reader accepts what we have said above about the various
aspects of dogmatic development.

Fifthly, we can now see where the whole crux of the matter
lies. For in the ante-Nicene period there was developing a new
mode of understanding, but this is something that cannot be
grasped by those who have never experienced a similar kind of
development themselves. Those who would have us employ
only the categories and the language of scripture, far from finding fault with the earliest Judaeo-Christians for resisting development, are in basic agreement with them. Those for whom
true knowledge is a matter of perception are at one with Tertullian, when they might have found in Tertullian the original
source of their error. Those who are afraid of intellectually
developed consciousness, or who are all in favour of some other
kind of truth, while branding propositional truth as mere
nominalism or a product of a mythic mentality, or who see in
dogmas the beginning of a metaphysics that they abhor, will
find in the Nicene dogma not a happy solution to difficult

[9] The topic of heuristic structures received fuller treatment in *Insight*, chapter
II; and cf. pp. 392–396.

problems, reached with the assistance of the Holy Spirit, but an aberration or, at best, a lamentable necessity arising out of a particular past situation.

Sixthly, we can see the usefulness of what we have to say in these pages. For those who have not been sufficiently helped by philosophical studies to develop, to purify, and to perfect their own capacity for understanding, can be helped by a concrete historical investigation, that not only shows how dogmas, in their original emergence, came to be properly understood, but also suggests the manner in which one can come to understand them properly today.

SECTION II

THE JUDAEO-CHRISTIANS

1. Judaeo-Christianity means different things to different people: some conceive it narrowly, as a complex of heresies arising out of Judaism; others think of it rather as a cultural form proper to what is called later Judaism, shared by the ortho-dox Jewish Christians no less than the heretics, and finding expression also in the writings of non-Jewish authors of that period.[1]

2. According to the former conception, Judaeo-Christianity is subdivided into various sects. J. Daniélou lists the Ebionites, the Elkesites, Cerinthus, the Christian-Samaritan Gnostics, various Gnostic sects in Egypt, and Carpocrates.[2] The Ebionites[3]—to take one example—declared their faith in Jesus Christ, but for

[1] The former conception is exemplified in J. Duplacy, *Lumière et Vie*, fasc. 29, 1956, 703–718, the latter in J. Daniélou, *Théologie du judéo-christianisme*, Tournai-Paris, Desclée, 1958. Daniélou writes (p. 19): "In this work Jewish Christianity should be understood to refer to *the expression of Christianity in the thought-forms of Later Judaism*". See A. Grillmeier, "Hellenisierung-Judaisierung des Christentums als Deuteprinzip der Geschichte des kirchlichen Dogmas", *Scholastik* 33 (1958), 321–355; 528–558. [Hereafter I shall refer to the English translation of Daniélou's book, mentioned in this note: *The Theology of Jewish Christianity*, translated and edited by John A. Baker. London, Darton, Longman & Todd, Ltd., and Chicago, The Henry Regnery Company, 1964. The sentence quoted above appears on p. 10 of the translation. *Trans.*]

[2] Cf. J. Daniélou, *op. cit.*, pp. 55–85.

[3] For a discussion of the Ebionites and of Ebionite sources, of how much is known about them, of disputed questions, and of their relationship to the sect at Qumrân, cf. J. Fitzmyer, *Theological Studies*, 16 (1955), 336–350.

them he was no more than a man who had a special call from God;[4] they left out of account the whole soteriological doctrine of the New Testament; they had, apparently, no teaching about the Holy Spirit, beyond what was already contained in the Old Testament; and they held on to the observance of the old law.[5]

3. However, if one thinks of Judaeo-Christianity not as a complex of heresies, but rather as a cultural form, one has a wider range of sources, and one also has to make one's entry into an unfamiliar world, with its own particular type of imagination, its own strange manner of conception and mode of speech. As well as the apocryphal books of both the Old and the New Testament, one takes account of the *Odes of Solomon*, the *Letter of Barnabas*, Hermas, Ignatius of Antioch and Clement of Rome, and all that Papias or Ireneus ascribe to the traditions of the elders.[6] To understand these texts correctly one must have some grasp of the literary genre, especially that of apocalyptic, to which they belong, and of the particular type of exegesis they contain.[7]

4. As a concrete illustration, we may take the following short passages from Origen:

"The Hebrew master used to say that the two Seraphim, whom Isaiah describes, each with six wings, calling out to each other and saying, *Holy, Holy, Holy Lord of Sabaoth*, were to be understood as the only-begotten Son

[4] In the *Clementine Homilies* (Altaner, 83 f.) Simon Magus argues that he who comes from God is God, but Peter replies that he cannot affirm any such thing, since he did not hear it from the Lord. *Hom. Clem.* XVI, 15; B. Rehm (GCS 42), 225, 15–18; MG 2, 377 B; cf. *ibid.*, from c. 11.

[Lonergan refers in this note to one of the many editions of B. Altaner, *Patrologie*, Freiburg, Herder. Hereafter I shall refer to *Patrology*, translated from the German by Hilda C. Graef, Freiburg, Herder and Edinburgh–London, Nelson, 1960. The reference here is to p. 104 f. of the translation. *Trans.*]

[5] J. Daniélou, *op cit.*, p. 63 f. For a very brief treatment of the Elkesites, see below, p. 111. On the other groups, cf. Daniélou, *loc cit.*

[6] J. Daniélou, *op. cit.*, pp. 7–54.

[7] *Ibid.*, pp. 87–115.

of God, and the Holy Spirit. For our part, we think that what is said in the canticle of Ambacum [Habac. 3, 3]: *In the midst of the two living creatures you shall be known*, is also to be taken as referring to Christ and the Holy Spirit."[8]

"For the Hebrew master also used to say as follows: the beginning or the end of all things can be known only by the Lord Jesus Christ and the Holy Spirit; that is what Isaiah expressed through his vision, in which there were only two Seraphim who *with two of their wings covered the face* of God, *with two others cover their feet and with two fly, calling out to each other and saying: Holy, Holy, Holy Lord of Sabaoth, the whole earth is filled with your glory*".[9]

Daniélou[10] compares with these passages the following, taken from St. Ireneus' *Proof of the Apostolic Preaching:*

"This God, then, is glorified by his Word, who is his Son forever, and by the Holy Spirit, who is the wisdom of the Father of All. And their powers (those of the Word and of Wisdom), which are called Cherubim and Seraphim, with unfailing voice glorify God, and the entire establishment of heaven gives glory to God, the Father of all".[11]

5. In *The Shepherd of Hermas* there is frequent mention of a certain angel, most worthy of veneration (ἄγγελος σεμνότατος), who sent the shepherd to Hermas,[12] and by whom all are said to be justified.[13] It would appear that this angel is to be identified with the glorious angel (ἔνδοξος) who grants the gift of prayer, and also with the Lord, mentioned immediately thereafter, who bestows the gift of understanding.[14] Moreover, it is the angel

[8] Origen, *De principiis*, I, 3, 4; Koetschau (GCS 22), 4–10; that it is not life (ζωή) but living creature (ζῷον) that is meant would appear to be established from a comparison of this passage with a preceding one: see Koetschau 52, 2, and critical apparatus.

[9] *De princ.*, IV, 3, 14 (26); Koetschau 346, 11–17.

[10] J. Daniélou, *op cit.*, p. 138.

[11] J. Smith, *St. Irenaeus, Proof of the Apostolic Preaching*, p. 10; ACW 16; London, 1952.

[12] *The Shepherd of Hermas, Vis.* V, 2; M. Whittaker (GCS 48), 22, 10 f.

[13] *Mand.*, V. 1, 7; Whittaker, p. 30, 10.

[14] *Sim.*, V, 4, 4; Whittaker, p. 56, 7, where the reading ἔνδοξος is preferred.

full of glory that determines who should suffer in this life;[15] and it is the same angel that shortly thereafter is called the angel of the Lord.[16]

In the *Eighth Similitude* there is a description, mostly in the language of apocalyptic symbolism (crown, seal, white robe, palm branches etc.) of the angel of the Lord, full of glory, who is extremely tall and who distinguishes between the good and the bad, crowns the just and leads them into the Church of the Saints.[17]

In the *Ninth Similitude* we read: "Did you see those six men and in the midst of them a man of great stature, full of glory (ἔνδοξος), going around the tower and rejecting stones from it? That man, full of glory, is the Son of God, and the other six are angels full of glory, accompanying him on the right hand and on the left. Without him none of those angels full of glory approaches God; and no one who has not received his name will enter into the kingdom of God".[18]

Here there are six, instead of seven, principal angels, whence perhaps it arose that Michael, the leader of the heavenly army (ἀρχιστράτηγος), was identified with the Son of God,[19] and Gabriel was sometimes identified with the Holy Spirit,[20] sometimes with the Word.[21]

6. There are similar conceptions in the *Ascension of Isaiah*:

"And I saw how he mounted to the seventh heaven, and all the just and all the angels glorified him. Then I saw him sitting down at the right hand of the Great Glory, whose brilliance, as I told you, I could not bear to

[15] *Sim.*, VII, I. 2. 3; Whittaker, p. 76. 16.
[16] *Sim.*, VII, 5; Whittaker, p. 65, 5.
[17] *Sim.*, VIII.
[18] *Sim.*, IX, 12, 7, 8; Whittaker, p. 86, 21-27.
[19] This is the more common view among scholars; the argument for it is based on many pieces of evidence. See *Sim.*, VIII, 3, 3; Whittaker, p. 68, 21; Daniélou, *op cit.*, pp. 127-131.
[20] Daniélou, *op cit.*, pp. 127-131.
[21] Daniélou, *op cit.*, p. 131 f.

behold. And I also saw the angel of the Holy Spirit sitting down on his left. And this angel said to me: Isaiah, son of Amos, I now dismiss you. . . . return into your vesture until your days are fulfilled. Then you shall return here".[22]

"And I saw one standing, whose glory surpassed that of all the others—his glory was great, and a wonder to behold. And . . . all the angels drew near and adored and sang. And the angel said to me: he is the Lord of all the splendours that you have seen. And while he was still speaking to me I saw a second glorious being, similar to the first, and the just drew near to him too, and adored and sang . . . . And I saw the Lord and a second angel, and they were standing; but the second angel that I saw was standing to the left of the Lord. And I said, Who is he? And the angel said to me: Adore him, for he is the angel of the Holy Spirit, who is upon you, and who has spoken also in the rest of the righteous".[23]

7. In Origen and Ireneus, in Hermas and the *Ascension of Isaiah*, we have found the term "angel" applied to both Christ and the Holy Spirit. J. Barbel illustrated this usage abundantly;[24] the inference drawn by M. Werner was that the Judaeo-Christians considered Christ a creature;[25] W. Michaelis[26] vigorously attacked Werner's interpretation and was supported in this by G. Kretschmar.[27] For the representation of the Blessed Trinity according to the vision of Isaiah (Is 6, 2 ff) recognises three distinct, subsistent persons, far more excellent than all the other angels. It is important to be aware that here we are dealing with categories that are semitic, not hellenistic: the hellenistic mind makes a sharp conceptual distinction between creature and creator, whereas the semitic does not, and so from the application to Christ of the term "angel" one must not infer that he was therefore regarded as a creature.[28]

[22] *The Ascension of Isaiah*, XI, 32–35; Daniélou, *op cit.* p. 129.

[23] *The Ascension of Isaiah*, IX, 27–36; Daniélou, *op. cit.*, p. 128 f.

[24] J. Barbel, *Christos Angelos*, Bonn, 1941.

[25] M. Werner, *Die Entstehung des christlichen Dogmas*, Leipzig, 1941, pp. 302–389.

[26] W. Michaelis, *Zur Engelchristologie im Urchristentum*, Basel, 1942.

[27] G. Kretschmar, *Studien zur frühchristlichen Trinitätstheologie*, Tübingen, 1956.

[28] J. Daniélou, *op. cit.*, p. 118.

8. *The exegesis of Genesis 1, 1*[29]

Clement of Alexandria, adducing in support the *Kerygma of Peter*, took the opening words, "In the beginning", to mean "In the first-born" and therefore in the Son.[30] According to Jerome, Aristo of Pella in his *Dialogue of Jason and Papiscus* translated the Hebrew thus: "In his Son God made heaven and earth".[31] Ireneus, giving first the Hebrew text, then translated: "A Son in the beginning God established, then heaven and earth".[32] Tertullian was acquainted with a similar rendering, but he considered it dubious: ". . . There are some who say that in the Hebrew text Genesis begins, In the beginning God made himself a Son".[33] Hilary, finally, says: "Breshith is a Hebrew word, which has three meanings: in the beginning, in the head, and in the Son".[34]

More recently, C. F. Burney offered the opinion that St. Paul had expounded three different meanings of the Hebrew word, *reshíth*, in teaching that Christ was "before all", "the head of the body, which is the Church", and "the first-born of all creation" (Col 1, 15–18).[35]

Certain Gnostics—Ptolemy, for instance—identified "the beginning" with the Son, and so they understood the Word as coming from the Son.[36] Justin, however, took the Word, the Beginning, and the Son to be one and the same;[37] for Tatian

[29] J. Daniélou, *op. cit.*, pp. 166 ff.
[30] Clem. Alex., *Strom.*, VI, 7, 58, 1; Stählin (GCS 15), 461; (cf. VI, 5, 39, 2), 451.
[31] Jerome, QQ. *herb. in Gen.*, I, 1; ML 23, 937.
[32] Iren., *Proof.* . . ., 43; Smith, p. 75.
[33] Tert. *Adv. Prax.*, 5; translation by E. Evans, London, SPCK, 1948, 93, 9 f.
[34] Hilar., *Tract. Ps.*, II, 2; ML 9, 263 A.
[35] C. F. Burney, *Journal of Theological Studies* 27 (1926), p. 175 f. Cf. Davies, *Paul and Rabbinic Judaism*, pp. 150–153.
[36] Iren., *Adv. Haer.*, I, 8, 5; W. W. Harvey I, 76; cf. I, 18, 1; Harvey I, 169, where we are told of a certain Gnostic who discovers the thirty Aeons in the first chapter of the book of Genesis.
[37] Just., *Dial.*, 61. 1; 72, 4. Note that it is established by other texts that Christ is the Beginning, e.g. Col. 1, 18; Rev. 3, 14 (cf. 3. 21); Prov. 8, 22; John 8, 25.

the "beginning" was the power of the word;[38] Theophilus of Antioch understood what was said of the "beginning" to apply to the Word;[39] for Origen the "beginning" was our Saviour and Lord Jesus Christ, the first-born of all creation, the Word, and he also said that Christ is the beginning, inasmuch as he is Wisdom.[40]

9. The Law and the Covenant[41]

The Law, νόμος, torah, is understood in an active sense—not as a legal document, but as God establishing laws. In Philo, λόγος and νόμος are identified.[42] Clement of Alexandria testified, however, that in the *Kerygma of Peter*, which is Judaeo-Christian, Christ is also called both *Logos and Nomos*.[43] Clement himself then cites Isaiah 2, 3 ". . . from Sion will go forth the law, and the word of the Lord from Jerusalem".[44] In *The Shepherd of Hermas*, while Christ is never called Logos, still the Law of God and the Son of God are identified with each other.[45] In Justin, Christ is sometimes called both the law and the covenant,[46] but sometimes he is only called the covenant.[47]

10. The Son is the name of the Father

In the earlier stages of culture, by "name" is normally meant not the mere name, but the person, the power, the nature of the

---

[38] Tatian, *Orat.*, 5.

[39] Theophilus, *Ad Autol.*, II, 10.

[40] Origen, *Hom. Gen.*, I, 1; W. A. Baehrens (GCS 29), 1, 9; *In Joan.*, I, 29; E. Preuschen (GCS 10), 23, 19.

[41] Daniélou, *op. cit.*, pp. 163 ff.

[42] Philo, *De Josepho*, 174; *Quaest. Gen.*, 4, 140; *De plant.*, 8 according to mss.

[43] Clem. Alex., *Strom.*, I, 29; Stählin II, 112, 5; MG 8, 929 A.

[44] Clem. Alex., *Eclog.*, 58; Stählin III (GSC 17), 154, 15; MG 9, 728. Ireneus demonstrates the application of Is. 2, 3 to Christ, *Adv. Haer.*, IV, 34, 4; Harvey II, 271 f.

[45] Herm., *Sim.*, VIII, 3, 2; Whittaker, p. 68, 18 f.

[46] Justin, *Dial.*, 11, 2; 24, 1 (according to the punctuation of ms. C); 43, 1; 122, 5.

[47] Justin, *Dial.*, 51, 3; 118, 3.

one named. Thus, "the name of God" meant to the Hebrews more or less what the divine οὐσία meant to the Greeks.

Now there is some evidence that the primitive Church, scrutinising the Old Testament in search of appropriate texts, did not neglect those passages where there is mention of the name of God. Thus Amos 9, 11 f, Isaiah 52, 5 and Exodus 9, 16 are cited in Acts 15, 16 f, Romans 2, 24 and Romans 9, 17, respectively.

Besides, while the texts in the Acts of the Apostles that speak of salvation through the name of the Lord (2, 21) or through his name (4, 12) perhaps refer rather to the divine nature of Christ than to a person distinct from the Father, Romans 10, 12 f suggests that it is one and the same thing to invoke the Lord (namely, Christ), and to invoke the name of him from whom salvation comes.

Moreover, in the Johannine writings one can perhaps discover a theology of the name. For the prayer, "Father, glorify your name" (John 12, 28) and the prayer "And now glorify me, Father" (John 17, 5), would seem to be one and the same prayer, and then the inference can be drawn that the Son is the name of the Father. Again, the words "I have manifested your name" can mean: I have manifested myself, who am your name. And so J. Daniélou asks: "Is it not possible that the expression: 'The Word ... dwelt among us' may be based on an older form: 'The Name ... dwelt among us'? In the Old Testament such dwelling is in fact the property of the name, and not of the Word".[48]

Clement of Rome, who does not call the Son Logos,[49] calls for obedience to the most holy name, full of glory,[50] and for submission to the omnipotent and most excellent name;[51] he com-

---

[48] Daniélou, op. cit., p. 150, n. 15; cf. p. 156; Didache X, 2: "We give thee thanks, O Holy Father, for thy holy Name which thou hast made to tabernacle (κατεσκήνωσας) in our hearts"; Jer. 7, 12; E. Peterson, Eph. lit., 58 (1944), .5 But J. Ponthot disagrees, Eph. theol. lov., 35 (1959), 339–361.

[49] Daniélou, op. cit., p. 151.

[50] Clem. Rom., Epist. I, 58, 1.

[51] Ibid., 60, 4.

mends confidence in the most sacred name of his magnitude,[52] the passage from ignorance into the knowledge of the glory of his name,[53] and hope in his name as in the source of all creation.[54] Here the final phrase suggests, perhaps, that in Clement "the name" means the Son, since τό ἀρχεγόνον πάσης κτίσεως ὄνομα is close to the phrase: the Word, that was the beginning, through which all things were made.

We may refer also to *The Shepherd of Hermas*, where we read that the tower (the Church) is founded on the word (ῥήματι) of the name that is omnipotent and full of glory, but is ruled by the invisible power of the Lord (δεσπότου);[55] that the name of the Son of God is great and infinite (ἀχώρητον) and carries the whole universe;[56] and it is asked, if the whole of creation is carried by the Son of God, what is to be said of those who have been called by him, those who bear the name of the Son of God and walk in his commands.[57] With this in mind one can understand Ireneus when he speaks of "The Lord manifestly coming into his own (domain) and his own (created nature) sustaining him while being itself sustained by him".[58]

The Gnostic writings contain very clear evidence of this archaic theology. For what is visible in Jesus is called Wisdom and the Church of the higher seeds ... what is invisible, however, is the Name, which is the only-begotten Son.[59] And so in a discussion of Matthew 22, 20 ("Whose is the image and superscription?") it is said that he has as a superscription through

[52] *Ibid.*, 58, 1.

[53] *Ibid.*, 59, 2.

[54] *Ibid.*, 59, 3.

[55] Herm. *Vis.*, III, 3, 5; Whittaker, p. 11, 3 f.

[56] Herm., *Sim.*, IX, 14, 5; Whittaker, p. 88, 22.

[57] *Ibid.* Cf. *Sim.*, IX, 13, 23; Whittaker, p. 87, 4 ff, from which it appears that "to bear the Name" means simply to be baptised. There is also a whole series of texts that link the Name with "sealing", with baptism, with the blessing of bread or oil, and with suffering for the Name. See Daniélou, *op. cit.*, pp. 153–157.

[58] Iren., *Adv. Haer.*, V, 19, 1; Harvey II, 375.

[59] *Excerpta ex Theodoto*, 26, 1; Daniélou, p. 153.

Christ the Name of God, and the Spirit as an image.[60] And in the recently discovered *Gospel of Truth* we read: "Now the Name of the Father is the Son".[61] What would become of such a theology when elaborated in the Gnostic style can be seen in the alphabetical speculations recounted by Ireneus.[62]

[60] *Ibid.*, 86, 1. 2.

[61] *Evangelium Veritatis.* 37, 37 (Malinine-Puech-Quispel, Zürich, 1956), Daniélou, *op. cit.*, p. 158. A. Orbe, *Hacia la primera teología de la procession del Verbo*, Rome, Gregorian University, 1958, pp. 70 f, 78 ff.

[62] Iren., *Adv. Haer.*, I, 14, 1; Harvey I, 127–130.

THE GNOSTICS AND OTHER SECTS

1. The only form of Gnosticism that concerns us here is heretical Christian Gnosticism; we shall not, therefore, deal with hellenistic or Jewish Gnosticism, or with the Gnosticism which has been detected in the writings of the New Testament itself.[1]

According to K. Prümm, the inspiration of Christian Gnosticism is expressed in the following passage:

> "What they say is that before a man is baptized, fate rules his life; but once he is baptized, what the astrologers say about him does not, in fact, apply to him at all. For baptism is not only a washing which leads us into liberty, it also brings us knowledge (γνῶσις) of our former state and of what, through baptism itself, we have now become; knowledge of where we were, or were thrown, of whither we are heading and from what we have been redeemed, of the meaning of birth and of rebirth".[2]

Answers to these questions were provided by the Gnostics (1) within a general context, or horizon, established by their own cosmogony and soteriology, (2) by means of pseudo-symbolic speculation (3) supported by New Testament exegesis.

2. The general scheme, or context, is established roughly as follows. Because of the problem of evil, the Stoic conception of

---

[1] For a brief account of each of these four forms of Gnosticism see LTK IV, 1021–1024 (K. Prümm), 1024–1026 (K. Schubert), 1026–1028 (R. Schnackenburg), 1028–1030 (H. Rahner).

[2] *Excerpta ex Theodoto*, 78; MG 9, 694; Other editions of the *Excerpta*: O. Stählin, GCS 17, Clem. Alex., III, pp. 105–133; R. P. Casey, London, 1934 (Introduction, Notes, English translation); F. Sagnard, SC 23, Paris, 1948.

God as immanent in the world—as indeed the soul of the world —is rejected. What is affirmed is a transcendent God, who is unknown and, to a certain extent, unknowable. The origin of all the evils in the world is found in a fall from the divine order, and salvation is placed in the acquisition of knowledge (gnosis) of God. The main points of difference between the Gnostic and the Christian scheme of things are that the Gnostics make no mention of creation, they introduce a series of intermediaries between God and man, and they attribute both fall and redemtion to a kind of natural process, rather than free will. This last point, for example, appears in the distinction they make between the "hylics", who cannot be saved, the "pneumatics", who cannot but be saved, and the "psychics", who may or may not be saved.

3. We have described the Gnostic mode of thought and style of speech as pseudo-symbolic speculation. It is speculation, because it deals with matters of ultimate concern; it is symbolic, because it employs the categories of sense and the sensible to expound a doctrine of a higher order; and it is pseudo-symbolic, because it personifies abstract ideas and mixes them in with the categories of sense.

Thus, according to Ptolemy, the divine order, or the *Pleroma*, is constituted by thirty Aeons, in groups of eight (the Ogdoad), ten (the Decad) and twelve (the Dodecad), all of the thirty Aeons being enumerated in the order of their emergence. The Ogdoad consists of four pairs, or couples: The Abyss and Silence (Thought, Kharis); Intelligence (The Son, the Only-begotten, the Origin and Source) and Truth; Logos and Life; Man and the Church. Each of these couples was a union of the masculine and the feminine principles, and also of the active disposition and the underlying matter. The Abyss and Silence—in a manner to be understood according to a sort of psychological analogy— gave expression to the transcendence of the hidden God. But Silence was also thought—spontaneous, ungrounded thought— and so there arose Intelligence, as the Only-begotten Son of the Abyss and Silence, and as source of all the other Aeons. And

Truth was united with Intelligence. From the union of Intelligence and Truth there proceeded Logos and Life, and from these came Man and the Church. Then, from Logos and Life there came the Ten, and from Man and the Church came the Twelve.[3]

4. What is of most interest to us is that in this conception of the divinity we find not only procession, conceived according to a psychological analogy, but also a twofold consubstantiality—the first between the two members of a single couple, the second between successive couples of Aeons. The first type of consubstantiality is attested by Ireneus, in the following passage:

"But another one, a distinguished teacher among them, reaching higher and as if advancing into greater knowledge, explained the first four Aeons thus: Before all is the Proarche, beyond all thought, ineffable and unnameable, whom I call Monotes (unity). With this Monotes is a power, and this I call Henotes (oneness). This Henotes and Monotes, being one, emitted, without emitting anything, the source of all things, intelligent, unbegotten and invisible. This source of all is given the name 'Monas'. With this Monad, in turn, there is a power that is consubstantial with it (δύναμις ὁμοούσιος αὐτῇ), which I call Hen (One). These four powers, Monotes, Henotes, Monas and Hen, emitted all the rest of the Aeons".[4]

We can notice here, in the first place, how the psychological analogy yields to a kind of fourfold unity. Secondly, the distinction of sexes, proper to the couples of Aeons, also disappears: Monotes, Henotes and Monas are feminine, and Hen is neuter, whereas, in Ptolemy's account, the Abyss (βυθός) is masculine and Silence (σιγή) feminine, Intelligence (νοῦς) masculine and Truth (ἀλήθεια) feminine. Thirdly, Monotes and Henotes are said to be one (τό ἕν οὖσαι). Fourthly, Hen is said to be consub-

[3] "Above all one must avoid taking this representation of the Pleroma too rigidly. The Aeons are intelligent emanations, pure spiritual (pneumatic) reflections, reflecting each other and merging with each other in the luminous unity of the divine Ocean." F. Sagnard, Clément d'Alexandrie, Extraite de Théodote (SC 23), p. 23. See Iren., Adv. Haer., I, 1, 1; I, 11, 1; Harvey I, 8 ff, 98 ff.

[4] Iren., Adv. Haer., I, 11, 3 (R. Massuet, MG 7); Harvey I, 102, 105.

stantial (ὁμοούσιον) with Monas. Fifthly, Monotes, Henotes, Monas and Hen are all called powers (δυνάμεις). Sixthly, the first two emit the others, and indeed, without emitting anything —which is a "dialectical" way of describing something that is like an emission, yet transcends the concept of emission.[5]

The second kind of consubstantiality, which should obtain between the one who emits and the one emitted, is attested by Ptolemy himself writing to Flora:

"Since, as we believe and profess, the Source of all things is one, un-generated and incorruptible, and also good; since, further, the good by its very nature generates and produces what is most like itself, and of the same nature as itself (ὁμοούσια); you may wonder how both of these natures can exist, namely, that which is corruptible and that which is in a kind of middle state, since they are different in nature from (ἀνομοούσια) what is incorruptible. Do not let this problem disturb you".[6]

Ptolemy promised that this difficulty would disappear as soon as Flora had heard a certain doctrine of the Saviour given to the Gnostics. Ireneus,[7] however, urged the same difficulty, and with justice, since the principle, that every agent produces its own like, cannot be reconciled with the successively lower ranking of the emissions, which was a central feature of the Gnostic system.

5. The ordinary sense of the word, homoousion, is illustrated in the Valentinian writings, where it is said that first there is made "a soul which is earthly, material, irrational, and consubstantial (homoousios) with the beasts;[8] but then the Demiurge breathes

---

[5] On contradiction as an expression of transcendence, see Orbe, op. cit., p. 14 f. For a commentary on the whole passage cited above, see A. Mendizábal, El Homoousios Preniceno Extraeclestiástico, Madrid, 1956, pp. 25-34.

[6] Epistula Ptolemaei ad Floram, in Epiphanius, Haer., 33, 7; MG 41, 567 B; K. Holl I (GCS 25), p. 457, 8-12; G. Quispel (SC 24), pp. 66 ff. For a comment-ary on this passage see Mendizábal, loc. cit., pp. 36 ff.

[7] The expression, of one substance, recurs, Adv. Haer., II, 17, 2, 3, 4, 5, 6, 7; MG 7, 762-764; Harvey I, 307-310. Cf. Orbe, op. cit., 660-663; Mendizábal, op. cit., 41 ff.

[8] Excerpta ex Theodoto, 50, 1.

into and sows in that soul something that is consubstantial with himself; its substance is called the spirit of life, and when the soul is formed by that substance it is made into a living soul.[9] Similarly, the cockle-seeds mentioned in St. Matthew's gospel (13, 25) are called the devil's seed, as being consubstantial with him. The matter becomes somewhat more obscure when the body of Jesus is said to be consubstantial with the Church.[10]

6. Having said something of the general scheme of the Gnostics, and of their peculiar type of speculation, it remains that we should give at least a very brief indication of their style of New Testament exegesis.

The *Pleroma* itself was considered to be the model, or exemplar, for the mystical union between Christ and the Church; as model or exemplar, it has to be manifested in an image, and this is what Paul had in mind when he said: "This is a great mystery, I mean in Christ and the Church".[11]

The "wedding garment" (Mt 22, 12), the comparison between the wedding feast and the kingdom of heaven (Mt 22, 2), and the fulness of joy of the bridegroom's friend (John 3, 29 f) were taken as hinting at the heavenly marriages, which were so much a part of the Gnostic system.[12]

As regards the Ogdoad, Ireneus tells how they found it all in the prologue to St. John's Gospel:

"Therefore, he first laid down a certain principle which was the first thing made by God, and this he also calls the Son and the only-begotten of the Lord, in whom the Father brought forth (emitted) all things seminally. They say that from him the Word was emitted, and in the Word the whole substance of the Aeons, which the Word itself afterwards formed.

[9] *Ibid.*, 50, 2, 3. On the underlying ontology, cf. Orbe, Index, p. 814, s.v. οὐσία.

[10] *Ibid.*, 42, 3. *Homoousia* appears also in 58, 1, in Sagnard's edition, but the reading is doubtful.

[11] Iren., *Adv. Haer.*, I, 8, 4; Harvey I, 75. Cf. Eph. 5, 32; to which one might readily add Eph. 5, 30 f; Gen. 2, 24; 1 Cor. 6, 15–17.

[12] All of these are mentioned in the *Excerpta*, 61, 8; 63, 1, 2; 64; 65, 1, 2.

And since he is talking of the first origin he rightly speaks of the beginning, that is, the Son, and the Word. For he says, *In the beginning was the Word, and the Word was with God, and the Word was God: this was in the beginning with God.* Having first distinguished the three, the Father, the Beginning, and the Word, he then brought them together again, in order to show the emission of both, that is, of the Son and of the Word, and their union both with each other and with the Father. For the beginning is in the Father and from the Father, and in the beginning and from the beginning is the Word. So he says well, *In the beginning was the Word,* for he was in the Son; *and the Word was with God,* also follows: for he was the beginning. *And the Word was God*: for what is born of God is God. *He was in the beginning with God,* shows the order of the emission. *All things were made through him, and without him nothing was made.* For the Word became the cause of the formation and generation of all the Aeons which come after him. *But what is made in him,* he says, *is life*: here he showed forth the couples: *For all things,* he says, *were made through him, but life was in him.* This life, therefore, which was made in him, is closer to him than those things which were made through him: for it is with him, and through him it bears fruit. For he adds, *And the life was the light of men.* He uses the same name for Man and for the Church in order to show the union of this couple. For of Logos and Life are born Man and the Church . . .".[13]

7. The Marcionites, the Manichees and the Mandeans all had a certain affinity with the Gnostics.[14] Marcion received his great illumination in the year 144; this was that God the creator, the God of the Old Testament who was a just and a rather harsh God, was not at all the same as the God of the New Testament. The defining characteristic of the God of the New Testament was his goodness: it was he who sent his Son (scarcely to be distinguished from himself) into this world, not so much to redeem us

[13] Iren., *Adv. Haer.,* I 8, 5; MG 7, 531–535; Harvey I, 75–78. Cf. *Excerpta ex Theodoto,* 6–8.

[14] On the leaders of the Gnostics, on Gnostic schools and documents, and on studies of Gnosticism by more recent authors, see Altaner, pp. 139–147. On the hellenistic and pagan cultural context, A. J. Festugière, *La Révélation d'Hermès Trismégiste,* 4 vols., Paris, 1949–1954. On the Valentinians, F. Sagnard, *La gnose valentinienne et le témoignage de S. Irénée,* Paris, 1947; G. Bardy, DTC XV (30), 2497–2519. On Gnostic trinitarian doctrine, A. Orbe, *op. cit.*

as to purchase us from the God of the Old Testament. Marcion did not take over the Gnostics' mythical speculations about the Aeons, but he instituted a kind of Higher Criticism of the Bible. To the God of the New Testament he attributed only St. Luke's Gospel—and then not all of it—and edited versions of most, but not all, of St. Paul's Letters. All the rest he attributed to the God of the Old Testament.[15]

Mani, Manes, or Manichaeus, as he is variously called, was born in Babylon about the year 215. His doctrine combined an Iranian and Babylonian mythology with some elements from the Old and New Testaments. It spread far and wide and was solidly established by skilful ecclesiastical organisation.[16]

The Mandeans, a smaller sect, still exist today. *Manda*, in Aramaic, means the same as *gnosis*, in Greek. Although their written documents are of a later age, their roots can be traced back as far as the second century, and perhaps even further, to some sort of contact with John the Baptist.[17]

8. From the time of Harnack it has frequently been said that the Gnostics were the first Christian theologians, since it was they who first used the psychological analogy, and the notions of consubstantiality and of procession. What is one to make of such an assertion? In the first place, we must note that there is a great difference between the dramatico-practical pattern of experience, common to all men, and the intellectual, or theoretic, or scientific pattern of experience (think of Thales, so intent on the stars that he fell into the well). Further, the drive towards theory has first to develop and become manifest, before one can learn how to guide and control it by logic, by scientific method, and so on. So the cult of numbers preceded the science of mathematics, astrology preceded astronomy, alchemy pre-

[15] G. Bardy, DBS V, 862–877; E. Amann, DTC IC (18), 2009–2032.

[16] G. Bardy, DTC IX (18), 1841–1895; J. Ries, "Introduction aux études manichéenes. Quatre siècles de recherches", *Eph. theol. lov.*, 33 (1957), 453–482; 35 (1959), 362–409.

[17] J. Schmitt, DBS V, 758–788; G. Bardy, DTC IX (18), 1811–1824.

ceded chemistry, legend preceded history and theogony preceded theology. Viewed from this point of view, what happened when heretics borrowed some elements of the Christian faith should cause no great surprise, but one does not have to call the resulting speculation Christian theology.

SECTION IV

ADOPTIONISTS, PATRIPASSIANS, SABELLIANS

1. The Adoptionists, as they were called, held that Jesus was a mere man, in whom God dwelt in a special way. The others whom we consider here did not deny the divinity of Christ, but they did away with the distinction of persons in God. They themselves took pride in the name of Monarchians, but the Christians called them Patripassians or, from the name of one of their leaders, Sabellians.

2. Hippolytus tells of a certain *Theodotus* of Byzantium, who acknowledged God as creator, but held that Jesus was a mere man, though born of a virgin according to the divine will. In Theodotus' view, when Jesus was baptized in the Jordan he did not become God, but he received the power to work miracles, because a certain spirit, who is the heavenly Christ, descended upon him in the form of a dove, and dwelt within him.[1] Some of Theodotus' disciples added that after his resurrection Jesus did in fact become God; and a second Theodotus, gilding the doctrine of his master, said that the heavenly Christ was the image of a supreme power named Melchisedech.[2]

According to Eusebius, there was a certain *Artemas* who also taught that Jesus was a mere man, claiming that this doctrine of his was nothing new, since it was the doctrine of the Apostles

---

[1] Hippol., *Refut.*, VII, 35; P. Wendland (GCS 26); MG 16³, 3341 c.
[2] *Ibid.*, 3344 A.

themselves and also, until the death of Pope Victor (about 198), of the Bishops of Rome.[3] Artemas' followers—perhaps he himself—held Euclid, Aristotle, Theophrastus and Galen in the highest esteem; they are said to have found in the scriptures only examples of syllogisms.[4]

Again according to Eusebius, Origen, with great skill and wisdom, succeeded in converting *Beryllus of Bostra*, who "dared to assert that our Lord and Saviour, before he moved among men, did not subsist as a distinct person, and further, that in himself he had not his own, but only the Father's divinity".[5]

Paul of Samosata, bishop of Antioch from about 260 to 270, was condemned, in a synod held in that city, for his christological doctrine. Eusebius says that he revived the heresy of Artemas,[6] and Alexander, bishop of Alexandria, says of Arius that he taught the heresy of Ebion, Artemas and Paul of Samosata.[7] According to Epiphanius, it was the doctrine of Paul that there was one God, that the Word of God was not subsistent (ἐνυπόστατος), but was in God in the way in which a man's own reason is within him; and it was this Word of God that dwelt in Jesus.[8] There are other documents extant, but their authenticity is in dispute.[9] The Homoeousians, in the fourth century, claimed that the condemnation of Paul included a condemnation of the word, consubstantial.[10]

[3] Euseb., HE V.28; MG 20, 511 ff. In refutation of this view Eusebius appeals first to the scriptures, then to various Catholic authors, and finally to Victor himself, who excommunicated Theodotus. *Ibid.*, 514 A.

[4] *Ibid.*, 515 AB.

[5] Euseb., HE VI, 33; MG 20, 594 A.

[6] Euseb., HE VII, 27–30; MG 20, 706 ff.

[7] Alex., *Epist. ad Alex ep. Thess.*, Opitz, AW III, 25, 10 f.

[8] Epiphan., *Haer.*, 65; MG 42, 120 ff; K. Holl III (GCS 37) 3 f.

[9] Altaner, *op. cit.*, p. 241 f. Following the studies by F. Loofs, 1924, and G. Bardy, 1929[2]. H. de Riedmatten, *Les actes du procès de Paul de Samosate*, Freiburg (Switzerland) 1952. *Epistola sex epp.*, in Hahn, 178–182; Mansi I, 1033 ff; B. Xiberta, *Enchiridion de Verbo Incarnato*, Madrid, 1957, 93 f.

[10] G. Prestige, *God in Patristic Thought*, London, 1936, pp. 201–209, has shown that this condemnation was differently explained by Athanasius and Basil, on the one hand, and on the other, by Hilary. Cf. A. Orbe, *op. cit.*, p. 678 f, note 11.

3. *Praxeas*, known to us only through Tertullian's work of refutation, *Against Praxeas*, did away with the distinction between the Father and the Son; he also attacked the Montanists. And so Tertullian writes: "Thus, in Rome, Praxeas accomplished two things for the devil: he expelled prophecy and brought in heresy, drove out the Paraclete and crucified the Father".[11]

Noetus of Smyrna likewise denied the distinction between the Father and the Son. He was attacked by Hippolytus, both in his *Against the heresy of Noetus*[12] and in his *Refutation of all heresies*.[13]

Sabellius was excommunicated by Pope Callistus.[14] He became influential, either directly or indirectly, in the Pentapolis of Libya, and his influence provoked the intervention of Dionysius, bishop of Alexandria, to which we shall have to refer again.

Hippolytus gives the following description of a doctrine which had spread through Rome:

"... saying that the Logos himself is the Son, and that the same is also given the name, Father; that in fact, however, there is only the one undivided Spirit; that the Father is not one thing and the Son another, but that both are one and the same; that all things, both the higher and the lower, are filled with the divine Spirit; that the Spirit, clothed with flesh in the Virgin, is not something different from the Father, but that both are one and the same. And that that is the meaning of the saying, 'Do you not believe that I am in the Father, and the Father in me?' What is visible, namely, the man, is the Son, but the Spirit who came down on the Son is the Father; for, he says, I profess faith in one God, not two. For the Father, who exists in him, having taken on flesh, deified what was now united with him and made it one with himself, so that the Father and the Son are called one God; and this person, since it is one person, cannot be two persons, and so the Father suffered together with the Son ...".[15]

[11] Tert., *Adv. Prax.*, 1.

[12] Hippol., *C. Noet.*; also P. Nautin, *Hippolyte, Contre les hérésies*, Paris, 1949; cf. Altaner, 185 (Syntagma).

[13] Hippol., *Refutatio* IX, 7 and 10; P. Wendland (GCS 26), 240, 242; MG 16³, 3369 D, 3377 AB. Cf. Epiphan., *Haer.*, 57; MG 41, 995 D ff.

[14] Hippol., *Refutatio*, IX, 12; Wendland, 248, 18; MG 16³, 3384 B.

[15] Hippolytus attributes this doctrine to Callistus himself, but he calls it the error of both Sabellius and Theodotus. Catholic scholars consider the accusation

Epiphanius says that the doctrine of the Sabellians distinguished, in the one God, three names, or three activities. He uses two similes: as in one man the body, the soul and the spirit are distinguished, so in God, the Father is like the body, the Son is like the soul, and the Spirit is the divine spirit. Again, as in the sun we distinguish its round shape, its power of illumination, and its power of heating, so, in God, the heat is the Spirit, the light is the Son, and the form of the whole substance is the Father.[16]

The pseudo-Athanasius found an affinity both with the Stoics and with Sabellius in those "who think that God contracts, and then expands with created things, and that he is infinitely at rest.... The Unity, by expansion, became the Trinity.... from which it follows that the Father himself became both the Son and the Holy Spirit, unless the unity which he proclaims is something other than the Father".[17]

---

against Callistus ungrounded, because (a) Hippolytus himself testifies that Callistus excommunicated Sabellius and (b) his great antagonism towards Zephyrinus and Callistus is manifested in the many other charges he levelled against them. Cf. G. Bardy, *Monarchianisme*, DTC X (20), 2193–2209. See also Altaner, p. 185, on Nautin's disputed opinion on the authenticity of the *Refutatio*.

[16] Epiphan., *Haer.*, 62, 1; K. Holl II (GCS 31), p. 389; MG 41, 1052 BC.

[17] Ps.-Athan., *Orat. 4 c. Arianos*, 13; cf. 25; MG 26, 483 f; 506. Cf. Dionysius, bishop of Alexandria, "Thus we expand the indivisible unity into Trinity and then we contract the Trinity, which cannot be diminished, into unity". In Athan., *De sent. Dion.*, 17; MG 25, 506; Opitz, AW II, 58, 24 f. Quite clearly, as long as one is confined within naive realism, and so incapable of effectively transcending the sphere of images, one can interpret this same image either in a Sabellian sense or in the sense of Tertullian. On the other hand, as soon as one begins to reason about true propositions, as in Ps.-Athanasius, the absurdity of the Sabellian opinion becomes manifest. For further comments on Sabellianism see A. Orbe, *op. cit.*, pp. 22, 579, 620, n. 18; 627, n. 25; 731, n. 29.

SECTION V

SUBORDINATIONISM

1. There are many conclusions, drawn from more recent theology, which, to those who are not very well versed in the matter, can seem rather subtle.

For example, the scriptures represent the Father as the one who is hidden, whom no one has ever seen, and the Son as the one who reveals him. If, however, one were to infer from this that the Father is invisible and the Son visible, one would be going against the doctrine of the consubstantiality of the Father and the Son. For if there is only the one divine substance, then either it is invisible or it is visible. And therefore, if the Father is invisible, it follows of necessity that the Son is also invisible.

Again, in the scriptures the Father is the one from whom all things come, whereas the Son is the one through whom all things come (1 Cor 8, 6; Col 1, 17; Heb 1, 3; Jn 1, 3). Besides, the Son is the Word (Jn 1, 1.18), the wisdom of God (1 Cor 1, 24), the image of God (2 Cor 4, 4; Col 1, 15); and one may add from the Old Testament whatever is said of wisdom (Prov 8, 22 ff) and of the creative word of God (Ps 32, 6; Gen 1). But if one were to infer from such passages that the Son was born of the Father only when the Father willed to create, in order to assist the Father in creating and governing the universe, one would be involved in many errors.

For the substance of the Father and that of the Son is one and the same substance; therefore, if the Father is eternal, so also is the Son. Again, if the Father exists for his own sake, not for the sake of his creatures, no less does the Son exist for his own sake.

And if the Father exists necessarily, then the Son exists necessarily. Further, just as the Father and the Son share the one substance, so in reality they also share a single will; and so the Son
cannot be some object, really distinct from the Father's will, and
arising out of a decision of the Father's will.[1]

Now these conclusions follow, beyond a shadow of doubt,
from more recent theology, but the ante-Nicene authors, to
judge from the language they used, had little grasp of them, and
so they have been charged with *subordinationism*.[2]

If the term, subordinationism, is used to describe a certain fact,
namely, that the ante-Nicene authors were not well up in the
theology of a later age, then of course its use is both legitimate
and useful. For before anything can be understood and explained, one must know precisely what it is that is to be understood and explained.

On the other hand, if we consider the proper goal of scientific
inquiry, which is understanding, then the term, subordinationism, becomes a source of the greatest obscurity and confusion.
For it is anachronistic to conceive the doctrine of the ante-Nicene
authors according to the criteria of a later theology, and anachronism precludes correct historical understanding.

It is for this reason that, when we come later on to deal with

[1] The council of Nicea says, DS 125, "God from God", and so the question
can arise whether one can also say, "substance from substance", "will from
will". [Cf. T. de Régnon, *Études de théologie positive sur la sainte Trinité*, Paris,
1898, III, 552 ff; Richard of St. Victor, *De Trinitate*, VI, 22 (Ribaillier, p. 259)].
To this question the fourth Lateran council replied in the negative, DS 804,
". . . that thing, namely, the divine substance, essence or nature . . . that thing
neither generates nor is generated, nor proceeds; it is the Father who generates,
and the Son who is generated, and the Spirit who proceeds . . .".

[2] Cf. G. Aeby, *Les missions divines de saint Justin à Origène*, Fribourg (Switzerland) 1958, who attributes a certain subordinationism to almost all of the ante-
Nicene authors. Thus, on Justin, p. 14 (cf. 7–14), on Tatian and Athenagoras,
p. 15 f, on Theophilus of Antioch, pp. 23 ff, on the Letter to Diognetus, p. 23,
on Tertullian, pp. 68 ff, on Hippolytus, p. 97 ("subordinationist climate"), on
Novatian, p. 106, on Clement of Alexandria, p. 130 ("links up with the subordinationist line"); A. Orbe, *op. cit.*, pp. 114 ff, seems to think St. Ireneus was
no exception.

the structure of the ante-Nicene movement,[3] we shall speak, not of subordinationism, but rather of a kind of dialectic, whereby firm belief in the revealed word of God gradually eliminated less exact conceptions, and thus prepared the way for the later theology.

[3] See below, p. 127

SECTION VI

"OF ONE SUBSTANCE"

1. Our next step will be to expound a mode of thought and expression which, while acknowledging that the Son is truly divine, does not at once eliminate all traces of subordinationism. It is found in its most fully developed form in Tertullian, but scholars use it also to characterise other ante-Nicene authors, in whom they detect a partial similarity to Tertullian, or some hints of a possible similarity, or at least no positive exclusion of such similarity.[1]

2. We have already referred briefly to Praxeas, who held that the Father and the Son were the same person. Tertullian composed his *Against Praxeas* as a defence of the following thesis: The Father is one [person], the Son is another, and both are the one God.

The reason why the Father and the Son are distinct from each other is that the Son is a substance emitted, or extruded, by the Father:

". . . . But I say that nothing could have come out of God which was empty and void, since that from which it was given out was neither empty nor void, and what proceeded from so great a substance, and made such great substances (for he also made the things that were made through him), was not itself without substance. Are we to imagine that he, without whom nothing was made, is himself nothing; that, himself being empty, he produced solid things, and himself being void, he produced full things and himself being incorporeal, he produced corporeal things? For, though it

[1] Cf. J. Lebreton, *op. cit.*; G. Aeby, *op. cit.*; A. Orbe, *op. cit.*

43

can happen on occasion that what is made is different from that which made it, nothing at all can be made through that which is empty and void. Is the word of God, which is also called the Son, and also called God— And the Word was with God, and the Word was God—is this word an empty and a void thing? It is written, you shall not take the name of God in vain. He indeed is the one who, being constituted in the form of God, thought it not robbery to be equal to God. In what aspect or form of God was he then? Certainly in some form or aspect, not in none: for who will deny that God is a body, although God is a spirit? For a spirit is a body *sui generis*, in its own form. And if those things which are invisible have, in God's presence, their own bodies and shapes, by which they are known to God alone, how much more shall that which was emitted from his own substance be not without substance. And so, whatever the substance of the Word was, that I call a person; and for that person I claim the name of Son and, acknowledging the Son, I hold that he is a second [person], other than the Father".[2]

This is as clear as could be. The Word of God is not empty and hollow, like a sound uttered by man; proceeding from so great a substance and making such great substances, it is itself a substance. But what sort of a substance is it? It is of course a spirit, but even a spirit is a body *sui generis*, in its own likeness; for the things that we call invisible have their own shape in God's presence, whereby they are visible to him. One may indeed ask how the substance of the Son, conceived in this way, can be one with the substance of the Father. Tertullian's reply is to compare his own concept of emission with that of Valentinus:

"Valentinus removes and separates his 'emissions' [προβολάς] from their source, so much so that an Aeon does not know its own father. At length it develops a great longing to know its father, but it cannot; indeed, it is almost consumed by and dissolved into the rest of the substance. As we explain it, the Son alone knows the Father. He revealed the Father's mind and heart; in the Father's presence he saw and heard all things; what he says is what the Father has commanded him to say; it is not his own will, but the Father's, that he has made manifest, having known the Father's

[2] *Adv. Prax.*, 7; E. Evans, 95, 30 ff (E. Evans, *Tertullian's Treatise against Praxeas*, London, SPCK, 1948). Cf. *Apolog.*, 21, 10-13; Orbe, *op. cit.*, p. 677, n. 11.

will intimately, having known it indeed from the beginning. For who knows what is in God except the Spirit who is in him? But the Word consists of spirit: spirit is, as it were, the body of the Word. The Word, therefore, being always in God, says, I am in the Father; and because he was always with God it is written, And the Word was with God. He was never separated from the Father, never other than the Father: For I and the Father are one. This is Truth's emission [προβολή], which safeguards the unity of God; for we say that the Son was emitted from, but not separated from the Father".[3]

Therefore, although the Son is a substance emitted, or extruded, from the substance of the Father, their intimate union of knowledge and love, and the non-separation of the Son from the Father, constitute them as one. To explain this non-separation Tertullian draws on familiar images, used also by the Montanists:

"For God brought forth the Word, as the Paraclete also teaches, as the root brings forth the shoot, as the spring brings forth the stream, as the sun brings forth the beam. And these manifestations are emissions [προβολάς] of those substances from which they proceed. And I would not hesitate to say that the shoot is the son of the root, the stream the son of the spring, the beam the son of the sun; because every source is a parent and everything that is brought forth from a source is its offspring. Much more is this true of the Word of God, who received the name of Son in the proper sense. But the shoot is not separated and removed from the root, nor the stream from the spring, nor the beam from the sun; neither is the Word removed and separated from God. Therefore, using these comparisons, I declare that it is my view that God and his Word, the Father and the Son, are two: for the root and the shoot are two things, but conjoined; the spring and the river are two manifestations, but undivided; the sun and the beam are two aspects, but they cohere. If one thing comes out of another, it is necessarily a second thing, different from that out of which it came, but it is not on that account separate from it. But where there is a second [person], there are two [persons], and where there is a third, there are three. For the Spirit is third, with God and the Son, as the fruit is third, coming from the root and the shoot, and the stream is third, coming from the spring and the river, and the point of light is third, coming from the sun and the beam. Nothing, however, is exiled from its source, from which it draws its

[3] *Ibid.*, 8; 96, 25 ff.

45

properties. This conception of the trinity, as moving out from the Father in closely connected sequence, is in no way opposed to the monarchy, and it preserves the order of the divine economy".[4]

This passage shows how much Tertullian's mind is tied to images: the Son is other than the Father because a substance is emitted, or extruded, from a substance, and he proceeded, or came out; God is one, however, because two things are conjoined, two manifestations are undivided, two aspects cohere, because nothing is exiled from its source, and because the phases are tightly-woven. Elsewhere he says:

". . . . as if thus also the one could not be all, since all are from the one, namely, through the unity of substance; while at the same time the mystery of the divine economy should be safeguarded, which of the unity makes a trinity, placing the three in order not of quality but of sequence, different not in substance but in aspect, not in power but in manifestation: all of one substance, however, of one quality and of one power, because the phases, the aspects, the manifestations, are all of the one God, in the name of the Father and the Son and the Holy Spirit. How the processions yield a plurality in God, without division, will be shown in the discussions that follow".[5]

". . . . we explain why they are not called two gods or two Lords, yet as Father and Son are two, and this not by separation of substance but by disposition of substance, when we declare that the Son is neither divided from nor separated from the Father, that he is other than the Father not in quality, but in phase, that although, when named singly, he is called God, this does not mean that there are two gods—by the very fact that he is called by the name, God, because of unity with the Father".[6]

". . . . the Sun and its beam are two things, and two manifestations of one undivided substance; so too are God and his Word, the Father and the Son".[7]

Thus Tertullian conceived the unity of God. Of the divine monarchy he has this to say:

---

[4] Ibid., 8; 97, 3 ff. Cf. Apologeticus, 21; EP 277; ML 1, 394.

[5] Adv. Prax., 2; 90, 38 ff.

[6] Ibid., 19; 112, 2b ff. Cf. Evans, pp. 50–58. M. Kriebel, Studien zur älteren Entwicklung der abendländischen Trinitätslehre bei Tertullian und Novatian, Ohlau i. Schl., 1932, pp. 95 ff. G. Prestige, op. cit., chap. V.

[7] Adv. Prax., 13; 104, 21 ff.

". . . . But I say that there is no power and dominion that is so much that of a single person, so much his alone, so much a monarchy, that it is not also administered by other persons, close to him, whom he has appointed as his officials. But if he who is the monarch has a son, and if the son is given a share in the monarchy, this does not mean that the monarchy is automatically divided, ceasing to be a monarchy. For the monarchy belongs principally to him by whom it was communicated to the son and, being exercised by two who are so closely united with each other, it remains a monarchy . . . But pay attention, I beg you, to the meaning rather than the sound of the words I use. A monarchy is overthrown only when another power, of equal condition and degree, and thus a rival, comes forward, as when Marcion introduces a second god, in opposition to the Creator, or when Valentinus and his followers, and Prodicus and his, bring in their many gods. Then indeed is the monarchy overthrown and the Creator destroyed".[8]

3. The next point is to grasp the difference between the meaning of the phrase, "of one substance", as used by Tertullian, and that of "homoousion", as used by Athanasius. For both Tertullian and Athanasius set out to establish the same thesis, namely that the Father is God, that the Son is also God, and that there is only one God. Equally, each of them makes use of images as a means of eliciting some understanding of this thesis. Athanasius, however, inquires so diligently, piously and soberly —to use the phrase of the first Vatican council—that his reason, illumined by faith, discovers the following rule: "All that is said of the Father is also to be said of the Son, except that the Son is Son, and not Father". On the other hand, Tertullian's mind is so immersed in the sensible that for him a spirit is a body *sui generis*; so confined is he to the sphere of the imagination that he explains the unity of the divine substance in terms of the concord of a monarchy, and a kind of organic undividedness and continuity.

However, it is not our purpose to blame the ante-Nicene Christian authors for lacking the philosophical development that would have enabled them to shift from a naive to a critical

---

[8] *Adv. Prax.*, 3; 91, 28 ff, and 92, 10 ff. Cf. Evans, pp. 6 ff.

realism, but rather to draw attention to the consequences of this lack. For it is not just that Tertullian had an inadequate conception of the unity of the divine substance; he even said some things that contradicted his own fundamental thesis. For he held that the Son was temporal: "There was a time when there was neither sin to make God a judge, nor a son to make God a Father".[9] He may also have held that the Father and the Son were not, each in the same way, the divine substance: ". . . for the Father is the whole substance, whereas the Son is something derived from it, and a part of it, as he himself professes when he says, For the Father is greater than I".[10] He also taught that the Son is subordinate to the Father: ". . . the one commanding what is to be done, the other doing what has been commanded".[11] These positions stand in clear opposition to the principal thesis. For if the Son is God, and God is eternal, then the Son also is eternal; if the Son is God, and God is the whole divine substance, then the Son also is the whole divine substance; if the Son is God, and God commands, then the Son also commands.

4. We have been discussing the difference between the position of Tertullian and that of Athanasius. It is not enough, however, to grasp this difference; the significant thing is to understand the movement, or dialectic, that brought about the development from the one position to the other. This dialectic is, indeed, the heart of the whole matter.

Within this dialectic we distinguish a material and a formal principal, the dialectic process itself, and the term, or goal, of the process.

The *material principle* is an objective contradiction, which may be either explicit or implicit.

The *formal principle* is the rational subject, under the aspect of his rationality, illumined either by the light of natural reason

[9] *Adv. Hermogenem*, 3; CSEL 47, 128, 5; ML 2, 199.
[10] *Adv. Prax.*, 9; Evans, 97, 34 f, and cf. note p. 245 ff; A. Orbe, *En los albores de la exegesis Johannea*, Rome, Gregorian University, 1955, p. 106, n. 13.
[11] *Adv. Prax.*, 12; 102, 15.

alone, or by the light of reason strengthened by the greater light of Faith.

The dialectic *process* is the actual elimination of the contradiction. For it is a natural tendency of reason to get rid of contradictions. If the contradiction in question is only implicit, it is first made explicit; then one side of the contradiction can be clearly affirmed and the other denied. Where reason is somewhat tardy, or the matter itself rather difficult, the process is gradual: one by one, different elements of the contradiction are made explicit, until eventually the whole contradiction is eliminated.

The *term* of the dialectic is either heresy or an advance in theology. It is heresy, where only the light of natural reason is operative; it is an advance in theology, where reason is illumined and strengthened by faith.

Applying these general categories to our present topic, we can say that in Tertullian we have found the material principle of a dialectic. For he held that the Father is not the Son, nor the Son the Father, and that both are God: but he also held that the Son was temporal; he made a distinction between the whole divine substance, on the one hand, and a derived portion of it, on the other; and he had the Father commanding what was to be done, and the Son doing what was commanded. A few simple syllogisms suffice to show that the latter assertions contradict the basic thesis. Secondly, the formal principle, as far as rationality itself is concerned, is common to all thinking men; as far as reason illumined by faith is concerned, it is present in all believers, considered precisely as believers. Thirdly, the dialectic process itself is grasped, not in any single author, considered apart, but in a whole series of authors, coming one after the other, each in his own way trying to resolve the basic contradiction, until at last it is in fact totally eliminated. Finally, the term of this dialectic, inasmuch as it is an advance in theology, we shall find in Athanasius; inasmuch as it is heresy, we shall find it in the Arians.

5. Tertullian's position was shared, more or less, by other ante-Nicene authors. Because he expressed himself more fully and more clearly, we have cited him at greater length; as the others were themselves more brief, so we may treat them more briefly.

6. We have already referred to Hippolytus' (died 235) refutation of Noetus. The heresy he found in Noetus was the same heresy that Tertullian had found in Praxeas.

The familiar images are there:

"... and, generating light from light, he sent him forth to the world as its Lord, his own mind (νοῦν). .... And thus there was another by his side But when I say that there was another, I do not mean that there are two gods; for the second is as light from light and water from a spring, or as a beam coming from the sun. For there is a single power that comes from the whole; the whole, however, is the Father, from whom there comes the power that is the Word".[12]

He explains that God is one because of the oneness of power:

"And if he wants to know how it is shown that God is one, let him know that the power or potency of God is one. As far as power is concerned, God is one; but from the point of view of the economy or disdisposition, there is a triple manifestation of power."[13]

The divine economy he describes thus:

"I shall not say that there are two gods, for there is only one; but I say that there are two persons; and the third economy I call the grace of the Holy Spirit [or with Nautin: but there are two persons in the economy; and the third is the grace of the Holy Spirit]. The Father is one, but because there is also the Son, there are two persons, and the Holy Spirit is the third. The Father commands, the Word carries out his commands: the Son is made manifest, and through him one comes to believe in the Father. The economy of concord comes back to one God, for there is one God, the

[12] *Contra haeresim Noeti*, 10, 11; MG 10, 817; EP 391 f; P. Nautin, [*Hippolyte, Contre les Hérésies, Fragment*, Étude et édition critique, Paris, 1949], 252, 9 ff.

[13] *Ibid.*, 8; MG 10, 816; Nautin, p. 249, 20. Heraclides likewise affirmed that the power of the Father and of the Son was the one power. *Entretien d'Origène avec Héraclide* ..., ed. J. Scherer, Le Caire, 1949, p. 124, line 6. Also SC 67.

Father, who commands; he who obeys is the Son; he who teaches knowledge is the Holy Spirit".[14]

In the *Refutation of all heresies* we read:

"Therefore this one God, who is above all things, first, by thinking, brought forth the Word; not a word like that which comes from the mouth of man, but rather an interior word, expressing his understanding of all things. He, the Word, is the only being generated by God; for the Father himself is the being from whom came that which was generated. . . . His Word is the only thing that comes out of him; therefore, he too is God, since he is God's substance. The world, however, came from nothing; therefore it is not God. . . .".[15]

7. Novatian, who died around the year 257, wrote a work entitled *On the Trinity*, in which he describes how, in a kind of circular movement, the power of the divinity, transmitted from the Father to the Son, is directed back again from the Son, into the Father:

"Hence all things are laid at his feet and delivered to him who is himself God, but, since he refers back to the Father everything that is subjected to him, he returns to the Father the whole authority of the divinity; and so the Father is the one true, eternal God, from whom alone the power of the divinity comes, which he transmits and extends to the Son. Because, being turned back into the Father, the Son shares his substance, the Son is also God, for to him the divinity has been extended; nevertheless, the Father is the one God; for in stages, by a backward flow, the majesty and the divinity, given by the Father to the Son, is turned back by the Son himself and returns to the Father".[16]

Novatian, however, used more than his imagination; to some extent he anticipated the later doctrine of relations of opposition in God:

---

[14] *Ibid.*, 14; MG 10, 821 A; Nautin, 255, 30 ff.
[15] *Refut.*, X, 33, 1 and 8; Wendland (GCS 26), 289, 3 and 290, 7; MG 16³, 3448 B and 3449 B.
[16] *De trin.*, 31; ed. Fausset [Cambridge, 1909], 122, 4 ff; ML 3, 852 AB. Cf. Orbe, *op. cit.*, 534 f.

" . . . . The Son is indeed a second divine person, God proceeding from God, but this does not mean that the Father is no longer the one God. If the Son had not been born but, like the Father, had known no birth, then they would both be equal, alike in all things, and thus there would be two gods. If he had not been begotten, then, comparing him with the Father, who is unbegotten, and finding them equal to each other in this, we would have to say that the two, both unbegotten, were two gods".[17]

Still, it cannot be said that Novatian reached an exact understanding of the matter. Rightly he asserts that the Father, neither born nor begotten, is the source, while the Son, born and begotten, comes from the source; at the same time, he says implicitly that the Father is invisible and incomprehensible, whereas the Son is both visible and comprehensible, and this is a position that cannot be maintained—for God is invisible and incomprehensible, and the Son is God. Further, in his reasoning about time, Novatian would have it that the Father was always Father; but he would also have it that he who had no origin or source should come before him who had.[18]

8. As well as Tertullian (against Praxeas) and Hippolytus (against Noetus) Dionysius, bishop of Alexandria, also launched an attack on Sabellianism, in a letter to Ammon and Euphranor. Dionysius himself, as we shall see later, received much milder treatment from Athanasius than he did from Basil, or from modern historians.[19] For in this letter, as both he and Athanasius admitted, Dionysius had written:

" . . . . that the Son of God is a work of God, a thing that was made, not by his own nature God, but other than the Father in respect of his substance; as the farmer is different from the vine, and the carpenter is different from the bench he makes. For since he is a thing that was made, he did not exist before he was made".[20]

[17] *Ibid.*, 31; Fausset, 119; MG 3, 949; EP 608.
[18] *Ibid.*, 31; ML 3, 950, 949. Cf. Orbe, 537.
[19] Basil, *ep.* 9; MG 32, 268; Hefele-Leclercq, *Hist. des conciles*, II¹, 344 ff. Orbe, 619.
[20] In Athanasius, *De sententia Dionysii*, 4; MG 25, 485 A; AW II, 48, 21.

Here we have so forceful a rejection of Sabellianism as actually to anticipate the doctrine of Arius. In fact, an accusation of heresy was brought against Dionysius in Rome, where the reigning Pope was another Dionysius. In reply to the accusation, Dionysius of Alexandria offered the defence that what he held ought to be gathered from all of his writings taken together, and that in other places he had asserted the contrary of what was now being held against him; that is to say, he had used the familiar images, in which it was possible to grasp some notion of consubstantiality.[21]

9. We also have from Athanasius the letter that Pope Dionysius sent to his namesake of Alexandria, in which he attacks both the Sabellians and the tritheists. While the Sabellians did away with any real distinction between the divine persons, the tritheists "destroy the monarchy, the most august doctrine in the preaching of God's Church, by dividing it and cutting it up into three powers, three separate hypostases, three deities" (DS 112). Against such separation, division, dissection, Pope Dionysius taught that "It must be maintained that the divine Word is united with the God of all things, and that the Holy Spirit remains and dwells in God; and so the divine Trinity is to be seen as one, brought together in its peak, as it were, in the omnipotent God of all things" (*Ibid*).

In this teaching of Pope Dionysius there are three things to be distinguished. First, he affirms beyond all doubt both that there is but one God and that the Father, the Son and the Holy Spirit are three, really distinct from each other. Second, there seems to be nothing new in his manner of conceiving the unity of God: rejecting all separation, division, dissection, he insists that the Word is united to the God of all things (the Father), that the Holy Spirit remains and dwells in God, and that the Blessed Trinity is brought together and brought back to its peak, in the God of all things. Third, although this conception of the divine unity lacks the perfection that came through later development,

[21] Cf. Orbe, *op. cit.*, 619.

it by no means leads to the conclusion that the opposing attributes of the Father and the Son are absolute, as they are in Tertullian and others.

10. Etymologically, the Latin word, *substantia*, corresponds to the Greek word, *hypostasis*, ὑπόστασις. However, where the Latins spoke of a single substance in God, the Greeks quite commonly acknowledged three hypostases. This is certainly true of a later period, but the usage goes back as far as Origen.[22] Arius held that there were three hypostases in God,[23] but so did Alexander of Alexandria,[24] who condemned Arius. It would seem, then, that George of Laodicea is expressing the common view when he explains that the Easterns affirm that there are three hypostases in order to safeguard the distinction of persons and not as if they were affirming that there were three gods.[25]

Marcellus of Ancyra, however, according to the testimony of Eusebius, held that there was one tri-personal, thrice-named hypostasis in God,[26] and Eusebius judged that this opinion was openly Sabellian. But whatever the truth is about Marcellus, the council of Sardica, in 343, gave some consideration to a formula, according to which the Father, the Son and the Holy Spirit share one hypostasis, or *ousia*, so that the hypostasis of the Son is the same as that of the Father, since there is only the one hypostasis in God.[27] Athanasius, however, denied outright that the council had actually approved the formula in question;[28] he himself was not willing to affirm either that there was only one, or that there were three hypostases in God; content to hold fast

[22] Orig., *In Joan.*, II, 10 (6); E. Preuschen (GCS 10), 65, 16.

[23] Arius, *Prof. fidei*, Opitz, AW III, 13, 7.

[24] Alexander, *Ep. ad Alex. ep. Thess.*, IX; MG 18, 561 B; AW III, 25, 23; here the Father and the Son are said to be "two natures in hypostasis".

[25] George L., in Epiphan., *Haer.*, 73, 16; Holl, III (GCS 37), 288 f.

[26] Euseb., *De eccl. theol.*, III, 6; E. Klostermann (GCS 14), 164, 26.

[27] In Theodoret, HE II, 8; MG 82, 1012 ff. Mansi, VI, 1215 ff. Hahn, § 157, p. 188. The formula was presented to the council by the presiding Bishop, Osius of Cordoba, Hefele-Leclercq, I², 748.

[28] Athan., *Tom. ad Antioch.*, 5; MG 26, 800 C.

to the decree of Nicea, he asked those who affirmed that there was only one hypostasis, whether they denied the distinction of persons; and he asked those who insisted that there were three hypostases, whether they meant that there were three gods.[29]

11. The extent to which the Latins grasped, or failed to grasp, the later meaning of the formula, "of one substance" is illustrated both by the outcome of the council of Rimini,[30] and by the rather lengthy explanations that Hilary gave of the difference between *homoousion* and *homoeousion*.[31]

---

[29] Athan., *ibid.*, 5 and 6; col. 801.

[30] See below, p. 79 f. Jerome more or less says that the bishops assembled at Rimini were inculpable because ignorant. *Dial. c. Lucif.*, 17 ff. ML 2.3, 170 ff.

[31] Hilar., *De synodis*, 67–77; ML 10, 525–530. Cf. P. Smulders, *La doctrine trinitaire de S. Hilaire de Poitiers*, Rome, 1944 [Analecta Gregoriana 32], pp. 235 ff.

SECTION VII

"THE IMAGE OF GOODNESS ITSELF"

1. Origen,[1] who laid great emphasis on the strict immateriality of God the Father,[2] also held that the Son was hypostatically distinct from the Father,[3] that he was the substantially subsisting wisdom of God the Father,[4] that he was absolutely incorporeal

[1] We now confront a new kind of problem, one that arises not from naive realism but from conceptualist or essentialist tendencies: the total transcendence of God the Father is acknowledged, but the difficulty in conceiving the Son is thereby increased. For if one acknowledges that the Son also is divine, and transcendent, one seems to be denying that he is distinct from the Father; on the other hand, if one asserts that the Son is distinct from the Father, one seems to be denying his transcendence. Jean Daniélou shows how troublesome this problem was from the time of the Apologists to that of Origen; see his *Message évangelique et culture hellénistique aux II* et *III* siècles*, Desclée & Co., Tournai, 1961, pp. 297–344. [*Gospel Message and Hellenistic Culture*, translated, edited and with a Postscript by John Austin Baker, London, Darton, Longman & Todd, Ltd., and Philadelphia, The Westminster Press, 1973, pp. 323–375. *Trans.*].

Origen died 254/55. Cf. Altaner, *op. cit.*, 223–235. G. Bardy, DTC XI (22), 1516–1528. A. Orbe, *Primera teología*, 165–179; 343–351; 674–692. J. Daniélou, *Gospel Message . . .*, 375–386. H. Musurillo, "The Recent Revival of Origen Studies", *Theological Studies*, 24 (1963), 250–263.

[2] *De princ.*, I, 1; Koetschau (GCS), 16–27; *In Joan.*, IV, 21 ff; Preuschen (GCS), 244 ff.

[3] "Therefore we worship the Father of truth and the Son who is the truth, two things [πράγματα] in respect of hypostasis, but one [thing] by harmony and concord and identity of will; in such manner that whoever sees the Son, who is the splendor of his glory and the figure of his substance, in him, who is the image of God, sees the Father also." *C. Celsum*, VIII, 12; Koetschau (GCS), 229, 31 ff; MG 11, 1333 C. Cf. Orbe, *Primera teología*, 431 ff.

[4] *De princ.* I, 2, 2; Koetschau, 28, 18.

and, in the strictest possible sense of the word, eternal,[5] that he was Son not by adoption, but by nature,[6] and that he was the invisible image of God.[7]

2. To some extent, Origen anticipated the rule of Athanasius, namely, that what is said of the Father is also to be said of the Son, except that the Son is Son, and not Father. For, since he conceived omnipotence as referring to an actual, rather than a possible, or futurible, exercise of power,[8] he could infer that as the Father made all things through the Son, so he was omnipotent through the Son,[9] and so both shared the same omnipotence. From this he drew the further conclusion that the words of Jesus, "Everything that is mine is yours, and everything that is yours is mine, and I am glorified in them", were to be taken to mean that whenever omnipotence is exercised, it is exercised by the Father and the Son alike.[10]

[5] *Ibid.*, Koetschau, 29. And *passim.*

[6] "For this eternal and everlasting generation is like the generation of brightness from light. For he does not become Son in an external manner, through the adoption of the Spirit, but is by nature Son." *De princ.*, I, 2, 4; Koetschau, 33, 1 ff.

[7] "In some such manner [namely, as an act of will proceeds from the mind] must we think of the Father begetting the Son, who is indeed his image; so that just as he himself is by nature invisible, so he has begotten an image that is also invisible." *De princ.*, I, 2, 6; Koetschau, 36, 1 ff. Cf. Orbe, *Primera teología*, 431 ff.

[8] Cf. the Greek words: παντοκράτωρ, πανταδύναμος. See *De princ.*, I, 2, 10; Koetschau, 41, 11 ff.

[9] ". . . for it is through the Son that the Father is omnipotent." *De princ.*, I, 2, 10; Koetschau, 43, 4.

[10] "However, that you may understand that the omnipotence of the Father and that of the Son is one and the same, just as God and the Lord is one and the same as the Father, hear how John speaks in the Apocalypse: 'These things says the Lord God, who is and who was and who is to come, the Almighty' (Rev. 1, 8). For who else but Christ is he who is to come? And just as no one ought to be scandalised because, the Father being God, the Saviour also is God, so too no one ought to be scandalised because the Father being called 'almighty', the Son also is called 'almighty'. Indeed it is in this way that we shall see the truth of what he says to the Father: 'All things mine are thine, and all things thine are

However, if we prescind from the consideration of divine attributes, this adds little to Hippolytus' conception[11] of the one power, common to the three persons of the Trinity, and it falls short of the universality of Athanasius' rule.[12]

3. Origen expounded the generation of the Son both negatively and positively. Negatively, he rejected any account that appealed to the analogy of human or animal generation,[13] and he characterised as absurd fables the kind of extrusions from the Godhead that some people pictured to themselves.[14] Positively, he said that the Son was the image of the Father, not in the sense that what is painted on wood or carved in stone is an image, but

".... in the way in which, according to the bible story, we say that Seth is the image of his father, Adam. For thus it is written: 'And Adam begot Seth according to his own image and likeness'. Image, in this sense, implies

---

mine, and I am glorified in them.' Now if all that belongs to the Father belongs also to Christ and if, as well as all else that he is, the Father is 'almighty', then without a doubt the only-begotten Son must also be 'almighty', so that everything the Father has, the Son may also have. 'And I am glorified in them,' he says. For 'in the name of Jesus every knee shall bow, in heaven and on earth and under the earth, and every tongue shall confess that Jesus is Lord in the glory of God the Father'. He is, therefore, 'the effluence of the glory of God' in this respect, that he is 'almighty'—God's pure, clear wisdom itself, glorified as being the 'effluence' of omnipotence or glory." De princ., I, 2, 10; Koetschau, 43, 10–27.

[11] See above, p. 50, n. 13.

[12] Athan., Orat. 3 c. Arianos, 4; below, pp. 101 ff.

[13] De princ., I, 2, 5; Koetschau, 32, 11 f.

[14] ". . . Let no one fall into the absurd fables of those who picture to themselves certain emanations, splitting the divine nature into parts and, as far as in them lies, dividing up God the Father. For even to begin to suspect that this could apply to an incorporeal nature is not only the utmost impiety but also the extreme in silliness; in no way is it consistent with intelligence to think that a physical division of an incorporeal nature is possible." De princ., I, 2, 6; Koetschau, 35, 10 ff. Cf. ibid., IV, 4, 1 (28); Koetschau, 349. In Joan., XX, 18; Preuschen, 351, 4 ff. In these latter passages Origen attacks those who say that the Son is from the Father's substance, on the ground that they thereby attribute bodily characteristics to God; the ante-Nicene Origen, therefore, understood the Nicene formula in a materialistic sense.

that the Father and the Son have the same nature and substance. For if 'everything that the Father does the Son does likewise', this means that in the Son there is formed the image of the Father; he is born of the Father, like an act of willing proceeding from his mind. And I think that the Father's willing something should be enough to make that thing subsist. For in willing, he wills only through the deliberation of his will. Thus, therefore, the subsistence of the Son also is generated".[15]

This passage is partly explained by Origen's conception of the one omnipotence of the Father and the Son, to which we referred above, but it requires some further explanation. For Origen held that the reason why the Son does not cease to be God is that he perpetually contemplates the profundity of the Father, and that the Son is what he is because of his constant acceptance of the Father's will.

"But again, the archetype of all images is the Logos, who is with God in the beginning, because he is with God and never ceases to be God; but he would by no means have remained God, if he had not remained in perpetual contemplation of the Father's profundity".[16]

". . . . and perhaps this is the reason why he is the invisible image of God: for the image that is in him is the image of the first will; and the divinity that is in him is the image of the true divinity. However, being also the image of the Father's goodness, he says, 'Why do you call me good?' For indeed, it is this will that is the Son's own food, and it is because of this food that he is what he is".[17]

The Son, then, is the image of the Father not only because he does everything the way the Father does, but also because he perpetually contemplates the Father's profundity and always follows the Father's will.

4. We are now in a position to locate Origen within the general dialectic that brought about a development in the manner of conceiving the Trinity.

[15] De princ., I, 2, 6; 34, 21 ff.
[16] In Joan., II, 2; Preuschen, 55, 4 ff; MG 14, 110 B.
[17] Ibid., XIII, 36; Preuschen, 261, 24 ff; MG 14, 461 C; the reference is to John 4, 34: "My food is to do the will of him who sent me".

In the first place, through his insistence on the strict immateriality of both the Father and the Son, he undermined every conception or theory which, unable to transcend the level of the senses, could think of the generation of the Son, and the unity of the Father and the Son, only in terms of "within" and "without", "separated" and "united", or other such spatial images.

Further, not only did Origen exclude every appeal to a material analogy; he also introduced a spiritual analogy. For he focussed attention on a procession which belongs to rational consciousness itself, within which, in his own words, "an act of willing proceeds from the mind". In some such way, he thought, we should conceive the Son's proceeding from the Father.

Origen's conception of this spiritual analogy is, however, different from that of later theologians, who had a precise grasp of the meaning of consubstantiality, and so admitted only one divine intellect, common to the Father, the Son and the Holy Spirit, and similarly, only one divine will. Origen, on the other hand, held that the Father knows himself much more perfectly than the Son knows him,[18] and that the will of the Son is only the image of the Father's will.[19]

The Father and the Son, then, are two hypostases, one of which, coming from the other, is related to its source as image to exemplar; these two hypostases, each in its own manner, create and maintain their mutual relationship, by understanding and willing. "This image", says Origen, "also contains the unity in nature and substance of the Father and the Son".[20] To come close to his meaning here, one may think of the highest form of Platonic participation, and think of it both as intellectual and as free.

---

[18] *De princ.*, IV, 4, 8 (35); Koetschau, 360, 4 ff; MG 11, 410. Cf. *In Joan.*, I, 27; Preuschen, 34, 19–31; MG 14, 74; here Origen says that the Son, being truth itself, knows all truth, but he suggests that there is perhaps a higher form of knowledge, proper to the Father, that transcends the notion of truth.

[19] See the reference in note 17, above.

[20] *De princ.*, I, 2, 6; Koetschau, 34, 23 f.

5. It will be well to say something about this notion of participation, which somehow pertains to the very notion of image itself.

For Origen ὁ Θεός and Θεός had different meanings, as had ὁ λόγος and λόγος. And so he thought that he had found a middle way between Sabellianism and Adoptionism, inasmuch as he held that the Father was *the* God, while the Son was God by participation, and was also the mediator through whom others were deified.

"Herein[21] lies the solution to the problem that disturbs many people who, professing their love for God, and fearful of saying that there are two gods, fall prey to false and impious doctrines, either denying that the Son is really distinct from the Father, because he whom they call the Son is only God with another name, or else denying the Son's divinity, saying that his nature and essence are quite different from the Father's.[22] To them we say that αὐτόθεος is indeed *the* God [God himself], which is why our Saviour, praying to the Father, says, 'that they may know you, the one true God'. Whatever else, other than him who is called αὐτόθεος, is also God, is deified by participation, by sharing [μετοχή] in his divinity, and is more properly to be called not *the* God [ὁ θεός] but simply God [θεός]. This name, of course, is his in a special way, who is the first-born of all creation, being the first to be with God, drawing the divinity to himself; he is more to be honoured in this name than the other gods there are besides him (they whose God is *the* God [ὁ θεός], according to the saying, 'The God of gods has spoken, and has summoned the earth') to them he gives being, drawing in abundance from God that whereby he might make them gods and give them help and support according to his own goodness".[23]

This style of thought, grounded in Plato's notion of participation, is applied by Origen not only to the divinity itself, as in the passage just cited, but also to other things. Sometimes the Son participates in what is proper to the Father; sometimes, however, the Son has something in his own right, than which the Father has something better. Thus, the Son is the true light, but the Father is as much above the true light as God, the Father of truth, is greater than truth itself, and the Father of wisdom is

[21] John 1, 1; Orig., *In Joan.*, II, 2; Preuschen, 54, 12 ff.
[22] On these distinctions, A. Orbe, *Primera teología*, 431 ff.
[23] *In Joan.*, II, 2; Preuschen, 54, 23 ff; MG 14, 110 AB.

more excellent than wisdom itself.[24] Again, Christ is life; but he
who is greater than Christ is also greater than life.[25] In the same
way, Christ is good, but the Father is goodness itself, good beyond all compare.[26] On the other hand, the Word is substantial
truth itself (ἡ ἀλήθεια ἡ οὐσιώδης) and substantial justice itself (ἡ
δικαιοσύνη ἡ οὐσιώδης) which, although not made *through* anyone, nevertheless are made *by* God the Father.[27] Indeed, Origen
understood the phrase, "The Father is greater than I" as having
universal application: the Son and the Holy Spirit are incomparably more excellent than all other things, but between them
and the Father, in turn, there is at least as great a gap, if not a
greater one.[28]

If we are to understand Origen properly, we have to appreciate how very different his whole way of thinking is from that
of the much later thomistic tradition, with which we are more
familiar. Thomists admit, of course, that "between the creator and
his creatures no similarity, however great, can be noted, which is
not coupled with an even greater dissimilarity" (DS 804). Still,
they do not say that the divine reality, inasmuch as it is beyond
the grasp of all created intellect, also transcends the very notions
of being, of essence, of truth, and of intellectual apprehension
as such, so that these notions cannot be applied to it at all. In fact,
whatever falls outside the range of being is nothing; and the
adequate object of intellect is being. But Origen favoured what
amounts to a negative theology—at times, admittedly, more by
way of speculation than of affirmation, but not in the passages
just cited, where he is, rather, deciding issues. He would appear
to be only speculating when he says that the God of all is simple,
invisible, incorporeal, and *either* mind *or* beyond mind and sub-

[24] *In Joan.*, II, 23 (18); Preuschen, 80, 12-15; MG 14, 156 A.

[25] *Ibid.*, XIII, 3; Preuschen, 229, 9 f.; MG 14, 404 C.

[26] *De Princ.*, I, 2, 13; Koetschau, 47, 3 ff; MG 11, 143 C; see also the passages
adduced by Koetschau, p. 46, 13, in critical apparatus.

[27] *In Joan.*, VI, 6 (3); Preuschen, 114, 22; 115, 1; MG 14, 209 D; cf. Orbe,
Primera teología, 441.

[28] *In Joan.*, XIII, 25; Preuschen, 249, 14 ff; MG 14, 411 B; *De princ.*, IV, 4,
8 (35); Koetschau, 360, 4 ff; MG 11, 410.

stance (οὐσία).[29] Equally, he is perhaps speculating when he asks whether we are to say, on the one hand, that the Only-begotten is the substance of substances (οὐσία οὐσιῶν), the idea of ideas, and the beginning, but on the other hand, that God his Father is beyond all these things.[30] He affirms without qualification, however, that the Son is truth itself, wisdom itself, the Logos itself, but that the Father is greater than truth and wisdom and life and Logos; and he even adduces as proof of the Son's eternity the apparent absurdity of saying that "there was a time when truth was not, when wisdom was not, when life was not".[31]

The point we wish to make is that there may be a kind of incommensurability between the whole mentality and the thought-categories of Origen and those of a later age, so that it would be unhistorical to transpose from the one to the other, as if there were an exact correspondence between them.

In our day we rightly make a very clear disjunction; either God or creature. If any creature is called God, we understand this only in the sense of a created, finite participation. But Origen does not assign to this disjunction the same fundamental and systematic function that we assign to it. It is said of the biblical mentality that its manner of apprehending everything is so concrete that it sees actions not only as manifesting, but also as constituting, the substances of things. Origen himself was a most diligent scriptural exegete, and not much of a metaphysician;[32] he too concentrated on the dynamic aspect of things, and particularly on freedom. Where we might speak of a universal principle of being, he would speak of all things coming *from* the Father and *through* the Son. For him, divinity and

[29] *C. Celsum*, VII, 38; Koetschau, 188, 11 ff; MG 11, 1473 B.
[30] *Ibid.*, VI, 64; Koetschau, 135, 9 ff; MG 11, 1396 D. Cf. *In Joan.*, XIX, 6; I, 27; Preuschen, 305, 16 f; 34, 19–31.
[31] *De princ.*, IV, 4, 1 (28); Koetschau, 350, 8–10; cf. 1, 1–3.
[32] "It cannot be brought out strongly enough that Origen himself was not a metaphysician in the proper sense of the word." Hal Koch, *Pronoia und Paideusis*, Berlin, 1932, p. 19. Cf. H. Crouzel, *Origène et la philosophie*, Paris, 1962, pp. 179–216, where the author attacks the opinion of those who held that Origen was a systematic thinker.

divinisation meant that the Father, whom no one has ever seen, was hidden, as it were, in the darkness of a negative theology,[33] and the Son, though he was Son by nature and not by adoption, nevertheless drew the divinity to himself by contemplating and willing. In the same way, the Son was to be called "the very stamp of his substance", not because he was of the same substance as the Father or like the Father in respect of his substance (*homoousios* or *homoeousios*), but because he enables others to understand and know God, revealing him to those to whom he chooses to reveal him.[34]

6. Mainly because of its relevance for the later Arian controversy, we must touch briefly on the question, whether or not Origen considered the Son a creature.

First of all, if we accept the version of Rufinus, the following passage is from Origen:

"For we do not say, as the heretics think, that some part of the Father's substance became the Son; neither do we say that the Son came from outside of the Father's substance, being created by the Father, so that there was a time when he was not. But, excluding every corporeal interpretation, we do say that the Word and wisdom were born, without any bodily process, of the invisible and incorporeal God, in the manner in which an act of willing proceeds from the mind. And thus it will not seem absurd, since he is called 'the Son of his love' (cf. Col 1,13), if in the same way he is considered the Son of his will".[35]

To which one may add: "For he does not become Son, from

[33] There is, however, a certain ambiguity in Origen's negative theology: the Father is placed beyond wisdom and truth; but wisdom (and perhaps truth) is conceived not in its full generality, but only as related to the actual world order. Still, the case of men like Philo, Origen and Pseudo-Dionysius is quite different from that of some modern authors (e.g. H. Duméry, *Le problème de Dieu*, Desclée, 1957) who, failing to exploit the well developed technique of analogy, place God outside the bounds of the intelligible order.

[34] Orig., *De princ.*, I, 2, 8; Koetschau, 38, 5-12.

[35] *De princ.*, IV, 4, 1 (28); Koetschau, 349, 3-10. Cf. Orbe, *Primera teología*, 398.

having not been Son, through the adoption of the Spirit, but is by nature Son".[36]

On the other hand, if we take Jerome's word, we are led to a different conclusion.

> "Candidus says that the Son is of the Father's substance, erring in this, that he asserts a προβολή, that is, an extrusion from the Father's substance. Origen, on the other hand, according to Arius and Eunomius, rejects the notion of his being extruded, or born, because this would suggest that the Father is divided into parts; what he says, rather, is that the Son is the highest and most excellent of creatures, and that he came into being through the Father's will, as did all other creatures".[37]

Now it is certain that verbally Origen called the Son κτίσμα and that he said that he was a creature; but so did many others, because they applied to the Son the passage in the book of Proverbs 8, 22.[38]

Secondly, to move from words to meaning, it is clear (1) that Origen always held that the Son was eternal, in the strict sense of the word; (2) that he affirmed that the Son was not made, and that he was the first-born of everything that was made (τὸν ἀγένητον καὶ πάσης γενητῆς φύσεως πρωτότοκον);[39] (3) that he said they were not to be listened to who inferred from John 1, 4 that the Word was made (γενητόν εἶναι τὸν λόγον);[40] (4) that he denied that the Son had a beginning, before which he was not (ἀρχὴν ... εἶναι υἱοῦ πρότερον οὐκ ὄντος.)[41]

Thirdly, there are no grounds for supposing that while the notion of consubstantiality developed only gradually, every-

---

[36] Ibid., I, 2, 4; 33, 2 f.

[37] Jerome, Apol. adv. Ruf., UU, 19; ML 23, 442 f. Cf. Orbe, Primera teología, 737.

[38] De princ., IV, 4, 1 (28); Koetschau, 349, 13–15. Origen's exegesis of this passage (Prov. 8, 22), ibid., I, 2, 2; Koetschau, 30, 2–8; that of Pope Dionysius, DS 114. On this whole question, D. Huet, MG 17, 768–790.

[39] C. Celsum, IV, 17; Koetschau, 88, 21 f.

[40] In Joan., fragm. 2; Preuschen, 485, 28; following the reading, "What was made in him, was life".

[41] De princ., IV, 4, 1; Koetschau, 349, 19 ff. But cf. ibid., I, 3, 3; 52, 1.

body always had a clear conception of creation. In fact, neither Plato, nor Aristotle, nor the Stoics, nor the Gnostics, had a doctrine of creation, in the strict sense of the word. Even the early Christians, who acknowledged the fact of creation, used the words ἀγέννητος (unbegotten) and ἀγένητος (not made) without discrimination;[42] and although Methodius and Origen, in the third century, introduced some clarity into the use of these two terms, the Arians, in the fourth century, re-introduced a kind of primitive obscurity and confusion.[43]

Fourthly, as Athanasius proposed a clear conception of con-substantiality, so he also had a clear and lucid notion of creation. For his distinction between creating and making is a profound one;[44] and he also established with precision the difference between being unbegotten and being created.[45] So he could argue effec-tively: If he is Son, he is not a creature; and if he is a creature, then he is not Son.[46] These clear ideas and sharp distinctions show plainly enough how closely connected are the two questions: Is the Son consubstantial with the Father? and, Is the Son a creature?[47]

Fifthly, if we accept this distinction, namely, that the Son is either consubstantial with the Father, or else he is a creature, then we must say that Origen's subordinationism, since it ex-cludes consubstantiality in the strict sense, also implies that the Son is a creature. However, this kind of implication, which in

[42] G. Prestige, God in Patristic Thought, pp. 37-52. J. Daniélou, Gospel Message . . ., pp. 324, 330 f.

[43] G. Prestige, ibid., p. 151 f. Prestige refers also to "the full examination of evidence", undertaken by himself, The Journal of Theological Studies, XXIV, 486; XXXIV, 258.

[44] Athan., De decretis nic. syn., 11; AW II, 9, 33 ff; MG 25, 433 C; the argument is based on the fact that God is ὁ ὤν, whereas men receive being from God.

[45] Athan., De synodis, 46; AW II, 271, 14 ff; MG 26, 776 B.

[46] Athan., De decretis nic. syn., 13; AW II, 12, 1 f; MG 25, 440 A.

[47] Cf. Athan., De synodis, 48; AW II, 272, 22 ff; MG 26, 777 C; the argument runs: if the Son is a creature, he is not consubstantial; and on the other hand, if he is truly Son, he is consubstantial.

fact is only an element of an objective dialectic, is not to be confused with a conclusion that somebody has actually drawn. The Arians drew such a conclusion, seeking to establish Origen as patron of their own position. So also did those who condemned Origen. But it is not at all clear that Origen either drew or could have drawn such a conclusion himself.[48]

---

[48] Apart from consubstantiality in the strict sense, there is another notion of consubstantiality, grounded in naive realism: from the substance of the Father there is emitted a substance of the same divine order, and this emitted substance would somehow constitute the real substrate of the Son. Thus Tertullian. In some such manner, according to A. Orbe (if I understand him aright), Origen also conceived consubstantiality. Cf. *Primera teología*, pp. 682, 401 ff, 441 ff. But as the distinguished author remarks, there would appear to be a lack of texts that would provide direct confirmation of this interpretation; thus, p. 441, note 49: "There are some passages that perhaps mean this"; also p. 682: "It is the most plausible explanation." However, the interpretation is not to be rejected on the grounds that Origen so clearly excluded all materiality from the Father and the Son; for the same Origen employed Stoic categories that contain implicitly not only naive realism but also a materialism. For a discussion of these categories see also Orbe, p. 439 f.

SECTION VIII

THE ARIANS AND SEMI-ARIANS

Arianism arose in Alexandria but spread rapidly. Before long it had the whole Eastern part of the Roman Empire in a state of turmoil that was to last nearly fifty years; then, having spread to the external proletariat it was transported by the conquering barbarians into the Western part of the Empire. In the earlier period there were three main phases. During the first phase, under the Emperor Constantine the First, who died in 337, stubborn defenders of the Council of Nicea were deposed from their episcopal sees, because of many and various accusations brought against them by the Arians. The second phase, under the Emperor Constantius, who died in 361, was marked by a plethora of minor councils and a multiplicity of creeds. In the third and final phase the faith of Nicea began to find general acceptance and within a short time was in fact universally accepted.

Although they share the same name, the Arians did not all share the same basic position. Arius himself held that the Son was a creature. But the followers of Eusebius, bishop of Caesarea, did not so much embrace the teaching of Arius as take a stand against the council of Nicea: they criticised the council for using non-scriptural language; they urged that the opinion of Marcellus, bishop of Ancyra, be accepted as the authentic exposition of the Nicene formula; and they themselves were content with the ambiguous doctrine of Origen, to which they appealed, namely, that the Son is, without difference, most like the Father. Then came those whom we may call the second-generation Arians: the *Anomoeans*, Aetius and Eunomius, who attempted a philosophically rigorous proof that the Son was a creature; the Homoeousians, such as Basil, bishop of Ancyra, who rejected the *homoousion* of Nicea, but held that the Son was truly Son, similar to the Father in substance (οὐσία) and in all things; and finally, the *Homoeans*, who said that the Son should be called the image of God, according to the usage of scripture, and that the very words οὐσία, ὁμοούσιον, ὁμοιούσιον, should be proscribed.

1. The roots of Arianism are traced back to *Lucian of Antioch*, founder of the exegetical school at Antioch, who favoured subordinationism, spent a long time outside of the Church but then apparently underwent a conversion, and died a martyr's death in 312. Arius and his first followers studied under Lucian, but what his own teaching was—or indeed, whether there were two Lucian's or only one—can be established only by laborious historical reconstruction. For the literature on the subject, see Altaner, p. 242.

2. *Arius*, an Alexandrian priest, having studied under Lucian, later became head of the exegetical school at Alexandria.[1] He publicly attacked the teaching of Alexander, bishop of Alexandria, for which, in 318, he was excommunicated by the synod of Alexandria. In spite of this, he continued to spread his own doctrine, and even managed to find favour with other bishops. So again he was condemned, first by the synod of Antioch,[2] in 325, and then, in the same year, by the ecumenical council of Nicea. He died in the year 336.

Of Arius' writings only the following are extant: (1) a letter to Eusebius, bishop of Nicomedia, written about 318;[3] (2) a profession of faith, in the form of a letter, sent to his bishop,

---

[1] Theodoret, HE, I, 1; MG 82, 885 A.
[2] Text in AW III, 36–41.
[3] In Epiphan., *Haer.*, 69, 7; Theodoret, HE I, 4; AW III, 1 ff.

Alexander of Alexandria, about the year 320;[4] (3) a profession of faith presented to the Emperor Constantine, towards the end of 327;[5] (4) a treatise entitled *Thaleia*, of which only fragments have been preserved;[6] (5) some other writings recently discovered, to which Altaner refers, p. 311.

Arius' letter to Alexander was signed by two bishops, six priests and six deacons. The profession of faith that it contains is as follows:

"This, blessed father, is the faith that we received from our elders, and also learned from you. We acknowledge one God, who alone is unbegotten, who alone is eternal, who alone is without beginning, who alone is true, who alone is immortal, who alone is wise, who alone is good, who alone is full of power; it is he who judges all, who controls all things, who provides all things; and he is subject to no change or alteration; he is just and good; he is the God of the Law and of the Prophets and of the New Covenant:

"This one God, before all time, begot his only-begotten Son, through whom he made the ages and the universe. He begot him not just in appearance, but in fact; by his own will he made his son to subsist and he made him unchangeable and unalterable. God's perfect creature, he is unlike any other creature; begotten, yes, but unique in the manner of his begetting:

"This offspring of God is not, as Valentinus taught, an emission of the Father; neither is he, as Mani taught, a part of the Father, consubstantial with him; neither is he the same person as the Father, as Sabellius said, dividing the unity; nor is it, as Hieracas held, as if there were one torch from another or one lamp with two parts. Neither is it true to say that he who previously existed was then begotten, or constituted as son: you yourself, blessed Father, many times, in council and in the midst of the Church, refuted those who held these views:

"But we say that he was created, by God's will, before all ages; from the Father he received being and life, and in creating him the Father conferred his own glory on him. Yet the Father, in giving all things into his possession, did not despoil himself of them: he contains all things in himself in an unbegotten way, for he is the source of all things. Therefore there are three substances (hypostases).

[4] In Athan., *De synodis*, 16; Epiphan., *Haer.*, 69, 7; Hilar., *De trin.*, 4, 12 f; 6, 5 f; AW III, 12 f.

[5] In Socrates, HE I, 26; Sozomen, HE II, 27; AW III, 64.

[6] In Athan., *De synodis*, 15.

"But God, who is the cause of all things, is absolutely the only one who is without beginning. The son, born of the Father before all time, created and constituted in being before all ages, did not exist before he was begotten: born outside of time, generated before all else, he alone received being from the Father. He is not eternal, co-eternal with the Father, nor is he, as the Father is, unbegotten; neither, as some say of things that are related to each other, does he have being simultaneously with the Father. For thus there would be two unbegotten principles. But God, as he is a unity (monas) and source of all things, so he exists before all things. Therefore he also exists before the Son, as we have heard you preach to the whole people. Inasmuch, then, as the Son has being, glory and life from the Father, in so much is God his source. He is his Lord, as being his God and existing before him.

"If some people understand the phrases *from him, from the womb* and *I came forth from the Father and I come* as implying that he is a consubstantial part of the Father, or a sort of emission, they make the Father composite, divisible and changeable; indeed God would be a body, if they had their way, and the incorporeal God would be affected in ways in which only bodies can be affected".[7]

We can gather from this that Arius and his companions wished to improve on the New Testament and the Apostles' Creed by excluding every metaphor and every anthropomorphism. The Father alone would be unbegotten, without any source, and eternal; the Son, because he has a source, would be neither unbegotten nor eternal, but would be a kind of supreme creature, made out of nothing through the will of the Father. Admittedly the phrase "out of nothing" does not occur in the long passage just cited, but Arius himself had earlier written to Eusebius of Nicomedia, a fellow-student of his at the school of Lucian, in the following vein:

"But what we say, and what we believe, is what we have taught, and still teach: namely, that the Son is neither unbegotten nor in any way a part of the unbegotten, and neither was he made from any pre-existing matter; by the decision and counsel (of the Father) he subsisted before all ages. He is fully God, God's only-begotten Son, and he is immutable; but before

---

[7] In Athan., *De synodis*, 16; MG 26, 707 ff. Orbe, *Primera teología*, pp. 727–737.

he was begotten, before he was created, before he was constituted in being by the Father, he did not exist. For he was not unbegotten. They persecute us because we say that the Son has a source and a beginning, but God has not. This is why they abuse us, and also because we use the phrase 'out of nothing' (*ex non exstantibus*); but we used this phrase because the Son is not a part of the Father, nor, on the other hand, was he made out of any pre-existing matter".[8]

Here Arius says that the Son is immutable, but on earlier occasions he had taught that he was mutable, according to the letter of Alexander of Alexandria, written to all the Bishops of the Church, about the year 319:

"The language they have invented, which runs counter to the meaning of scripture, is as follows:

"God was not always Father, but there was a time when he was not Father. The Word of God did not always exist, but was made out of nothing. For God, who is, brought into existence, out of what was non-existent, one who was non-existent, and so there was a time when he was not. For the Son is something created, something made. He is not similar to the Father in respect of substance (ousia); neither is he the true and natural Word of the Father, nor is he the Father's true wisdom, but belongs to the things that have been made and created. He is improperly called the Word and wisdom, since he himself was made through the word of God in the proper sense, and through the wisdom that is in God, in which wisdom God made not only all other things, but him as well. Therefore, he is mutable by nature, as all rational creatures are. The Word is outside of God's substance, other than God's substance, apart from God's substance. The Son cannot tell all about the Father; for he cannot see the Father perfectly, and his knowledge of the Father is imperfect and imprecise. Indeed, the Son does not even know his own substance, as it is in itself. For it was for our sakes that he was made, so that through his instrumentality, as it were, God might create us; and he would not have existed, if God had not wished to bring us into being. To the question, whether it is possible that the Word of God is such that he could be changed in the way that the devil was changed, they did not draw back from answering that it is indeed possible, because, being made and created, he is by nature changeable".[9]

[8] In Theodoret, HE I, 4; MG 82, 911 BC.
[9] MG 18, 573 AB; AW III, 7 f.

3. *Eusebius, bishop of Nicomedia,* who had enjoyed great influence at the court of the Emperor Licinius, was more a politician than a theologian. He was a friend and supporter of Arius, having been a fellow-student of his at the school of Lucian of Antioch. He died in 341 or 342. For editions and studies of his writings see Altaner, p. 240.

Among the extant writings of Eusebius there is a letter (written about 321–22) to Paulinus, bishop of Tyre, in which he said:

"We heard nothing, my Lord, about two infinite (unbegotten) beings; neither did we learn, nor do we believe, that the one infinite (unbegotten) being was divided in two, or that anything at all happened to him, that can happen only to bodies. There is one who is unbegotten, and one who is truly begotten of him, but not begotten of his substance, and in no way unbegotten. He was made, totally different in nature and in power, though constituted in a perfect likeness to the nature and the power of him who made him. We believe that the manner of his coming to be is not only beyond the power of words to express, but also beyond the capacity of any mind, whether human or superhuman, to grasp in thought. We are not affirming here what we have thought out for ourselves, but what we have learned from scripture. For we learned that he was created, constituted and born in his substance, in nature immutable and ineffable, and in the likeness of his maker, as the Lord himself says: 'God created me, the beginning of all his ways; before all ages he constituted me, and before all the hills he begot me' (Prov 8, 22). But if he had come out of the Father, in the sense that he was of the Father, namely, as a part of him or an outflow of his substance, then it would not be right to say that he had been established or constituted in being. . . .".[10]

Holding such a view, Eusebius—and with him four other bishops, Theognis of Nicea, Maris of Chalcedon, Theonas of Marmarica and Secundus of Ptolemais—was unwilling to subscribe to the formula of Nicea, because it contained the word *homoousion.* Socrates explains their reasoning thus:

"They said that 'consubstantial' applies to what comes out of something else, either as a part of it, or as an outflow, or as an eruption from it. By

[10] In Theodoret, HE I, 5; MG 82, 914; AW III, 16.

eruption, as shoots sprout from roots; by outflow, as children come from parents; by division, as two or three *philae* are taken from a lump of gold. In none of these ways, they asserted, did the Son of God come from the Father, and therefore they could not assent to that teaching. . . .".[11]

4. *Eusebius, bishop of Caesarea*, who died in 339, was a highly cultured and a very scholarly man; he is renowned for his *Ecclesiastical History* and his *Preparation for the Gospel*. Spiritual heir of Origen, Eusebius had a horror of all novelty. He was also a friend of the Emperor Constantine, on whom he lavished praise. While rejecting the doctrine of Arius, enshrined in the phrase "out of nothing", he also rejected the doctrine of consubstantiality, as propounded by the council of Nicea, because he considered it Sabellian. In the early stages of the Arian controversy he played a significant enough role; later on he and Acacius, who was to succeed him as bishop of Caesarea, became the leaders of the too-conservative Eastern bishops. For editions and studies of Eusebius' works, see Altaner, pp. 263–71.

Before the council of Nicea, in his *Demonstration of the Gospel*, Eusebius had written:

". . . . The Son was begotten, but not in the sense that at first he did not exist, and then came into existence: he existed before all time, proceeding from, and always present to the Father. He is not unbegotten, but begotten, the only-begotten Son of the unbegotten Father. He is from God, is God's Word, and is himself God. He was produced not by any kind of division of the Father's substance; but from all the aeons of eternity, or rather, before all the aeons of eternity, he was born, in a manner which it is beyond the power of words to express or of thought to conceive, of the ineffable and incomprehensible will and power of the Father".[12]

About the year 318, Eusebius explained to a certain Euphratio that the Father is distinct from the Son, and greater than the Son, in accordance with the saying in St. John's Gospel, 14, 28; that the Father is the only true God (John 17, 3), but that the Son is also God (John 1, 1), and the image of the one true God (Col 1, 15); that there is but one God, and one mediator between God

[11] Socrates, HE I, 8; MG 67, 68 f. Cf. Orbe, *Primera teología*, 660 ff.
[12] *Demon. ev.*, IV, 3; MG 22, 257; EP 668.

and man, the man Jesus Christ 1 Tim 2, 5). Eusebius concludes that the Father and the Son are not strictly simultaneous in being, but that the Father exists before the Son. For, he asks, if they were simultaneous in being, how could the Father be Father and the Son, Son, or the Father first and the Son second, or the Father unbegotten and the Son his only-begotten? For, on the supposition of their strictly simultaneous existence, either both would be unbegotten, or both begotten.[13]

At the synod of Antioch, in 325, Eusebius fell under grave suspicion of heresy and was warned that he must return to a proper frame of mind.[14] He took part in the council of Nicea and subscribed to the council's formulation of the faith, but not without feeling the need to write a long letter of explanation to his flock in Caesarea. On the phrase, "out of the Father's substance", he comments that, while the Son is out of the Father, he is not a part of the Father's substance; on the phrase "born, not made", he remarks that the word "made" is used to describe all the other creatures, which come into being through the Son, whereas the manner of the Son's generation is entirely different, and is beyond the power of words to describe. Finally, he explains the term "consubstantial" by saying that the Son comes out of the Father, not after the manner of bodily generation, nor by any division or dissection of the Father's substance, nor in any way that would imply that the substance or power of the Father undergoes any change, or any duplication, or is affected in any manner whatsoever; but the Son is like him who begot him, and like him alone, in every way, and he comes from no other hypostasis or substance. Eusebius adds, in conclusion, that the term "consubstantial" itself had been used before, by some eminent bishops and authors.[15]

That Eusebius inherited Origen's whole style of thought appears very clearly from his work, *On Ecclesiastical Theology*,

[13] Fragments of this letter are preserved in the acts of the second council of Nicea, Labbe 7, 365, 497; Mansi 13, 176, 317; AW III, 4 ff.

[14] AW III, 40, 5.

[15] AW III, 45; Socrates, HE I, 8; MG 67, 74; Athan., *De decretis,* 33.

which he wrote towards the end of his life, in 337–338. For example:

"We are constrained to acknowledge a single divine reality transcending all things, which is ineffable, good, simple, not composite, and one in form. This is God-himself (*autotheos*), mind-itself, word-itself, wisdom-itself, light-itself, life-itself, the beautiful-itself, the good-itself, and whatever else anyone might think of, greater than these things, and indeed, away beyond the power of any mind to conceive or words to express. We acknowledge also his Son, his only begotten, born of the Father as the Father's image, in all things most like to him who begot him. He is God and mind and word and wisdom and light and life, and he is the image of the good-and-the-beautiful-itself. He himself is not the Father, but the Father's only-begotten Son; he is not unbegotten, not without a source; he is born of the Father, and his source is he who begot him".[16]

5. *Asterius*, sophist and rhetorician, had, like Arius, been a student of Lucian of Antioch. He wrote various homilies, and commentaries on the Psalms, and a work entitled *Syntagmation*.[17] When Marcellus of Ancyra attacked him, both Eusebius of Caesarea (*Against Marcellus* and *On Ecclesiastical Theology*) and Eusebius' successor, Acacius, came to his defence. He died sometime after 341. See Altaner, p. 311 f., LTK I, 958.

Acacius consecrated St. Cyril as bishop of Jerusalem, enlarged the library at Caesarea, and led the *Homoeans* at the synod of Seleucia, in Isauria, in 359. He died in 366. Epiphanius has preserved some fragments of a work, written against Marcellus, in which, replying to the objection that the image of God is not God, and the image of the Lord is not the Lord, Acacius explains (1) that he is not thinking of a material image, but of a living, perfect image and (2) that the image of essence-itself (*autoousia*) also *is* essence-itself, and equally, the image of will-itself *is* will-itself.[18]

---

[16] *De eccl. theol.*, II, 14; MG 24, 928; EP 674; ed. Klostermann (GCS 14), 115, 15–26.

[17] Epiphan., *Haer.*, 72, 6–10; Holl III (GCS 37), 260–264; MG 42, 389–396.

[18] *Ibid.*, Holl, pp. 260, 19 ff; 261, 14 ff; 264, 10 ff. On editions and studies, Altaner, 271; LTK I, 234.

6. *Marcellus*, bishop of Ancyra, died about 374. He was a friend of St. Athanasius; he took part in the council of Nicea; and he wrote a refutation of the *Syntagmation* of Asterius. About the year 336 he was deposed by the Arians, who accused him of Sabellianism; Pope Julius, however, received him in Rome, and to Julius he presented a profession of faith. A disciple of Marcellus was Photinus, and the first canon of the first council of Constantinople contains a condemnation both of Marcellians and Photinians (DS 151). Klostermann collected the fragments of Marcellus' writings and published them in an appendix to his edition of Eusebius' works, *Against Marcellus* and *On Ecclesiastical Theology*.

In his profession of faith to Pope Julius, Marcellus first enumerates the errors of the Arians; then he affirms that the Son was neither made nor created, but is strictly eternal, without source, or, perhaps, beginning (ἀρχή), of his being; he affirms, further, that the divinity and the power of the Father and the Son are indivisible and inseparable from each other, since the Father is in the Son and the Son is in the Father; and explicitly he states that the reign of the Son is everlasting.[19]

The extant fragments of his writings reveal Marcellus as a systematic thinker, both in exegesis and in speculation. He draws a distinction between those New Testament texts that refer to the Only-begotten, and those that refer to the First-begotten; the former, he says, refer to the divine Word, the latter to the Word incarnate. The phrases, "the Son of God" and "the image of the invisible God", he applies to the Word incarnate, and also the other phrases that the Arians took in a subordinationist sense. The divine Word, however, is "the Word" and nothing else; if the scriptures seem to speak of the Son as eternal, the explanation is that he is predestined by the Father to be eternal (as in Romans 1, 4). There would also appear to be some elements of Sabellianism: the Word is in God from all eternity, but when the world was about to come into being, the Word came out of God as a kind of creative power; and so it is that the

[19] Klostermann, 215, 5–10, 25, 31. Or in Epiphan., *Haer.*, 72, 2, 3.

indivisible monad is expanded into a trinity. At the end of the world, however, the Word will go back into God, returning to the state in which it was before the constitution of the world.[20]

Photinus, who came from Ancyra in Galatia, was, as we have said, a disciple of Marcellus. He himself became bishop of Sirmium. Epiphanius describes him thus: going even farther than Paul of Samosata, not only did he deny that Christ existed from the beginning, but even said that he did not exist before Mary conceived of the Holy Spirit; from this he boldly concluded that the Spirit is greater than Christ; he admitted that the Word was eternally in the Father, but this he understood according to the analogy of a human word, denying that the Word was the Son.[21]

7. Those who were dissatisfied with the Nicene creed composed many rival creeds, in various places, at various times, and on various occasions, between the years 340 and 360.[22]

(1) The second council of Antioch, known as the Dedication Council, was held in 341. Four credal formulae are attributed to this council. Bardy (p. 122) thinks that the second of the four goes back to Lucian of Antioch, and he notes that the fourth did not emerge from the council itself, but was drawn up by four bishops a little later.[23]

(2) In 343, the Eastern bishops, refusing to enter into discussion with the "orthodox", who were gathered together in

[20] Fragm. (Klostermann), 3–14, 19, 32, 33, 41, 46, 52, 57, 60, 61, 67, 71, 72, 82, 83, 91–97, 103, 104, 117, 121. Cf. Orbe, *Primera teología*, pp. 622–633.

[21] Epiphan., *Haer.*, 71, 1, 2; MG 42, 374 ff; Holl III, 249, 251.

[22] See Athan., *De synodis*, MG 26, 681–793; Hilar., *De synodis*, ML 10, 471–545; the ancient Church historians: Socrates and Sozomen, MG 67; Theodoret, MG 82; Hahn, *Bibliothek der Symbole*, Breslau, 1897³; Hefele-Leclercq, *Histoire des conciles*, I, 2, 633, 987, Paris, 1947. P. Smulders, *La doctrine trinitaire de S. Hilaire de Poitiers*, Rome, 1944, Anal. Greg. 32.

[23] The credal formula is to be found in Hahn, §§ 153–156, and Athanasius §§ 22–25. See Smulders, pp. 22–24.

Sardica, withdrew to Philippopolis, where they held a council of their own and produced their own creed.[24]

(3) What is known as the Long-lined Creed, dating from the year 345, is an exposition of the faith prepared for the Emperor Constantius; four Eastern bishops brought it with them to Milan, where they sought to explain the Eastern theological standpoint to their Western colleagues and the Emperor Constans.[25]

(4) The first council of Sirmium, held in 351.[26]

(5) The second council of Sirmium, held in 357, produced a creed that Hilary called "the blasphemy of Sirmium".[27]

(6) The third council of Sirmium, held in 358, produced no new creed, but reaffirmed older ones, namely, those composed against Paul of Samosata and Photinus, and one of the creeds attributed to the second council of Antioch.[28]

(7) The bipartite general council, held at Rimini in the West and Seleucia in the East, is made up of many different episodes.

(a) The fourth creed of Sirmium, dated May 25, 359, was to be signed by all of the bishops, from the East and from the West alike. This was the emperor's way of preparing the ground for the council.[29]

(b) At Rimini, where more than 400 Western bishops had assembled, eighty Arians approved the fourth creed of Sirmium, on July 12, 359. The other bishops rejected it, and reaffirmed the faith of Nicea. Further, they excommunicated four bishops who were attached to the court of

---

[24] The credal formula of this council is to be found in Hahn, § 158, and Hilary, § 34. See Smulders, pp. 25 ff.

[25] Hahn, § 159; Athanasius, § 26; Smulders, p. 29 f.

[26] DS 139 f; Hahn, § 160; Athanasius, § 27; Smulders, pp. 32 ff.

[27] Hahn, § 161; Hilary, § 11; Smulders, p. 44.

[28] Sozomen, IV, 15; MG 67, 1152; Smulders, p. 52.

[29] Hahn, § 163; Athanasius, § 8; Smulders, p. 57.

the emperor, namely, Valens, Ursacius, Germinius and Gaius; and they sent a deputation of ten bishops to the Emperor himself.[30]

(c) At Niké, in Thrace, on October 10, 359, the delegates from Rimini were forced both to revoke the abovementioned excommunication and to subscribe to an ambiguously worded creed.[31]

(d) At Rimini, on the return of their delegates, the orthodox bishops, confused and deceived, submitted to the Emperor's demands.[32] It is to this that Jerome refers when he says: "The whole world groaned, astonished to find that it was Arian".[33]

(e) The Eastern bishops came together at Seleucia, from September 27 to September 30, 359. There the Homoeousians revived the second creed of the Dedication Council, hoping to have it endorsed by the assembly; the Acacians, for their part, attempted to impose their own formula.[34]

(f) Delegates from both sides, (Homoeousians and Acacians) sent to the Emperor at Constantinople, were given the choice of subscribing to an ambiguous credal formula, very similar to the one imposed on the Western bishops at Niké on October 10, 359, or of going into exile.[35]

8. We shall now present, in summary form, the main points of doctrine contained in the many credal formulae mentioned above.

[30] Smulders, p. 58 f.

[31] This formula is to be found in Hahn, § 164; Theodoret, 11, 16; MG 82, 1049; cf. Smulders, p. 59.

[32] Smulders, p. 60; cf. Hahn, § 166; Jerome, *Dialogue against the Luciferans*, 17; ML 23, 710.

[33] Jerome, *ibid.*, 19, col. 181.

[34] The Acacian formula is to be found in Hahn, § 165; Athanasius, § 29; cf. Smulders, p. 61 f.

[35] This formula is to be found in Hahn, § 167; Athanasius, § 30; cf. Smulders, p. 65 ff.

(1) *About Arius, or the doctrine of Arius*

The Dedication Council prefaces its first creed with the statement that its authors, being bishops, are not followers of Arius, a priest, and that, far from taking him as their teacher, they had received him back into communion only after rigorously testing his orthodoxy.

The second creed of the same council condemns those who, without warrant of scripture, acknowledge a time, or age, or moment before the generation of the Son. It also condemns those who hold that the Son is a creature, like any other creature, or that he was begotten in the way that others are begotten, or that he was made, in the way that other things are made.

The creed known as the fourth of Antioch, the creed of Philippopolis, and the first creed of Sirmium (in its first canon) all declare that: "The Holy Catholic Church dissociates itself from those who believe that the Son of God was made from nothing, or from some other substance, and is not of God himself; and that there was a time when he was not."

The Long-lined Creed contains (§ II) the same condemnation and (§ III) an explanation of it.

The first creed of Sirmium, in canon 13, declares those anathema who say that the divinity of our Lord was in any way affected by his passion.

(2) *About Marcellus or Photinus*

The third creed of Antioch teaches that the Son is perfect God of perfect God, existing in (his) hypostasis with the Father; it also explicitly anathematizes Marcellus, Sabellius and Paul of Samosata, and all who associate themselves with them.

The fourth creed of Antioch affirms that the Son shall reign forever and ever.[36]

The creed of Philippopolis condemns those who say that before all ages he was not the Christ, or was not the Son.

---

[36] Cf. C. A. Maly, *De Verbis symboli nicaeno-constantinopolitani "cuius regni non erit finis"*, Munich, 1939 (dissertation).

The Long-lined Creed (§ II) reiterates the condemnation contained in the creed of Philippopolis; it attacks the doctrine of Marcellus (§ V) and (§ VI) attacks both Marcellus and Photinus by name.

The first creed of Sirmium (canons 3 ff) proceeds implicitly against Marcellus and Photinus.

(3) *Ditheism and tritheism rejected*

The creed of Philippopolis anathematizes those who say that there are three gods.

The Long-lined Creed (§ II) teaches that the Father alone is unbegotten and without any source; it denies that the Son shares these characteristics with the Father; and it asserts that the source of the Son is the Father; for God is the head of Christ (§ III).[37]

Next, the same creed acknowledges three things (*pragmata*) and three persons (*prosopa*) in God, but it denies that there are three gods; it teaches that the Son, although subordinate to God the Father, is born of God before all ages and is, in respect of his nature, true and perfect God (§ IV). Finally, it proclaims that the Son, who is both subsistent and not separated from the Father, reigns harmoniously with the Father, in accordance with the traditional doctrine (§ IX).

The first creed of Sirmium (canons 2, 18, 26) denies that the Father and the Son are two gods, or that there are two who are unbegotten, or without source; for since God is the head of Christ, all things are reduced to the one source, which is itself without source.

The second creed of Sirmium, while affirming that the Son is born of the Father, as God from God and light from light, nevertheless strongly insists that there is but one God, and that the Father is greater than the Son in honour, dignity, glory, majesty and renown.

(4) That the Son is a) *Son*, b) *The only-begotten*, c) *God*, d) *He through whom all things are made*, is affirmed in the four creeds of Sirmium and the creeds (359–360) of Seleucia, Niké

[37] Cf. Euseb. Caes., *De eccl. theol.*, II, 7; Klostermann, 104, 18–25.

82

and Constantinople. The second creed of Sirmium ("the blasphemy of Sirmium") teaches that he is a) Son, b) born, begotten; it also teaches c) that there is one God of all, that the Son is manifestly not as great as the Father, but that he is nonetheless God of God, our Lord and our God.

(5) The doctrine that the Son is begotten *of the Father before all ages* is contained in the fourth creed of Antioch, the creed of Philippopolis, the Long-lined Creed, the first and fourth creed of Sirmium, and the creeds of Seleucia, Niké and Constantinople. The same teaching is expressed in equivalent terms in the first creed of Antioch. The second and third creeds of Antioch, and the second of Sirmium, contain the phrase, *before the ages*, but they omit the word, *all*.

(6) *The use of the terms* (a) *ousia*, (b) *homoousion*, (c) *homoeousion*, (d) *hypostasis*, (e) *substantia*, (f) *anomoeon*

The second creed of Sirmium excludes *ousia, homoousion, homoeousion* and *substantia*. The fourth creed of Sirmium excludes *ousia*; it teaches that the Son is similar to the Father in every respect.

At Seleucia, the Acacians excluded both *homoousion* and *homoeousion*, and *anomoeon* they labelled *anathema*; the formula they favoured was that the Son is similar to the Father, according to the Apostle (the image of God: 2 Cor 4, 4; Col 1, 15).

At Niké *ousia* is excluded; the Son is said to be similar to the Father, according to the words and the teaching of the scriptures.

(7) *No one understands, no one knows, the manner of the Son's begetting, except the Father who begot him*

Thus the fourth creed of Sirmium, and the creed of Niké and of Constantinople. The second creed of Sirmium teaches that only the Father and the Son know the manner of the Son's begetting.

(8) *The Son is from the will of the Father*

The creed of Philippopolis declares those anathema who deny that it was by a deliberate choice that the Father begot the Son. The Long-lined Creed (§ VIII) condemns those who teach that the Son was begotten without any decision of the Father's will: for the Creator himself did not beget (his Son) involuntarily; and the words of the Book of Proverbs (8, 22) are not to be ignored. At the same time, the begetting of the Son is to be clearly distinguished from the creation of everything else.

The first creed of Sirmium (canon 25) declares those anathema who say that the Son was begotten of the Father, without the Father's willing to beget him; for the Father was neither constrained, nor drawn by necessity of nature, to beget a Son against his will; but as soon as he wished, outside of time and without being in any way affected himself, he begot the Son out of himself.

(9) *The Son is a hypostasis distinct from that of the Father*

The second creed of Antioch teaches that there are three realities in God, in respect of hypostasis, but one reality by concord. The third creed of Antioch asserts that the Son, in (his) hypostasis, is with the Father. The Long-lined Creed simply rejects the mere phrase, not-existing-in-himself, having-being-in-another, whether indwelling in or being emitted from that other (§ V). The first creed of Sirmium (canon 8) declared anathema the notion of indwelling or emitted word ("*verbum insitum vel prolatum*"), and in many of its canons it inculcates both the unicity of God and the distinction of persons.

(10) Little is said in these creeds about how the distinction of persons is to be reconciled with the unicity of God; for the term *homoousion* is excluded. The second creed of Antioch and the Long-lined Creed speak of concord; the Long-lined Creed also speaks of a certain natural inseparability, the Father ruling and the Son subordinate to him. The first creed of Sirmium (canons 18, 26, cf canons 3, 27) teaches that the Son is subordinated to the Father.

9. The *Anomoeans* were a group of radical Arians, who asserted that the Son was *unlike* the Father. The outstanding figures

among them were Aetius and Eunomius who, introducing an Aristotelico-Stoic dialectic, and placing the essence of divinity in being unbegotten, concluded that the Son, as being begotten, could not be God.

Aetius, who lived from about 300 to 366, was born in Antioch. The Arians made him a deacon about the year 350, and a bishop about the year 362. He composed a work entitled *Syntagmation*, some chapters of which were reproduced,[38] and then refuted,[39] by Epiphanius.

Eunomius, who came from Cappadocia, was a disciple of Aetius. The Arians ordained him deacon in Antioch and later made him bishop of Cyzicus. Driven several times into exile, he died in Cappadocia between 392 and 395.

Eunomius pushed conceptualism so far that he taught that whoever has grasped the notion "unbegotten" knows God as well as God knows himself, thus taking up a much more extreme position than that of Arius, who held that even the Son did not know the Father. Further, erroneously reducing the basic principle of metaphysics, which affirms the correspondence of truth with being, to a conceptualistic disjunction, he asserted that either names are mere sound, signifying nothing, or else they express the very essences of things. Cf LTK III, 1182.

10. *The Homoeousians*, opposing both the Anomoeans and the Homoeans, held that the Son was similar to the Father in respect of his substance, and in every respect. The two most important documents are: 1) a declaration of the synod of Ancyra, held in 358, probably composed by Basil, bishop of Ancyra;[40] 2) a declaration by Basil of Ancyra and George of Laodicea, following on the fourth formula of Sirmium, 22nd May, 359, stating their position.[41]

[38] Epiphan., *Haer.*, 76, 11, 12; Holl III, 351–360; MG 42, 533–545.
[39] *Ibid.*, 76, 13–54; Holl, 360–414; MG 42, 545–640. Cf. LTK I, 165.
[40] Epiphan., *Haer.*, 73, 2–11; Holl, 268–284; MG 42, 404–425; Hahn, pp. 201–204, has the twenty anathemas that were appended to this declaration.
[41] *Ibid.*, 73, 12–22; Holl, 284–295; MG 42, 425–444. On Basil and George see LTK II, 31; IV, 702.

The declaration of the synod of Ancyra professes faith in the Father, the Son and the Holy Spirit, according to the baptismal formula; it affirms that the names, Father and Son, are not equivalent to the names, Creator and creature, respectively. While admitting that nothing can be said of God which implies any bodily attributes, it nevertheless confidently asserts that the Son is truly Son, similar to the Father in respect of his substance; and it urges that the objections usually brought forward against this view should be overcome not by argument, but by faith. Finally, it lays down twenty anathemas; these, for the most part, insist that the Son is truly Son, but the nineteenth anathema denies that the Father is, in his power or his substance, the Father of the Son, as it denies that the Son is consubstantial with the Father (homoousion), or is the same substance as (tautoousion) the Father.

The declaration of Basil and George, avoiding the use of the term, substance (ousia), teaches that the Son is similar to the Father in absolutely everything, and is therefore similar to him in respect of being. It also clarifies the term, hypostasis:

"But let no one be upset by the use of the term, hypostasis. For those in the East speak of hypostases when they wish to refer to the subsisting, existing, properties of the persons. For although the Father is a spirit, and the Son is a spirit, and the Holy Spirit is himself a spirit, we do not think that the Father is the Son. And indeed, the Holy Spirit himself subsists, and we by no means think of him as Son, since he is different from the Son. That Holy Spirit subsists through himself. For he is neither the Father, nor the Son, but the Holy Spirit, whom the Father, through the Son, bestows on the faithful. Therefore, as we have said, the Easterns call what is proper to the subsisting and existing Father, Son and Holy Spirit, the hypostases of the subsisting persons. It is not as if they were affirming that those three hypostases were three sources, or three gods: for they condemn those who affirm that there are three gods. Neither do they say that the Father and the Son are two gods. For this is what they profess: that there is one divinity which, through the Son and in the Holy Spirit, holds the universe; they confess one divinity, I say, one kingdom, one rule. Yet piously they distinguish the persons, in the properties of their hypostases: the Father, subsisting in his majesty as Father; the Son, not understood as a part of the

Father, but subsisting, and perfect, begotten of the perfect Father; and finally, the Holy Spirit, whom the sacred scripture calls the Paraclete, also subsisting, coming from the Father, through the Son".[42]

11. The *Homoeans*, as distinguished from the Anomoeans on the one hand, and the Homoeousians on the other, are a group who attempted a compromise (Acacius and his followers at the synod of Seleucia in Isauria, in 359), saying that the Son was similar to the Father, according to the Apostle. They gained the upper hand for a short time among the Greeks, and for a rather longer time among the barbarians, through the credal formulae of Niké and of Constantinople. Cf. Bardy, pp. 169 ff.

---

[42] Epiphan., *Haer.*, 73, 16; MG 42, 432 f. The declaration then cites 1 Cor. 12, 3; John 14, 9; Mt. 28, 19.

SECTION IX

HOMOOUSION, CONSUBSTANTIAL

1. The term, homoousion,[1] or consubstantial, is both philosophically and theologically ambiguous. Philosophically, the ambiguity arises from different views of human knowing: for what one means by οὐσία, or substance (and thus by *homoousion*, or consubstantial), will depend on whether one thinks that it is known by sense, or only through true judgment. The theological ambiguity, which presupposes the doctrine of the Trinity, lies in this, that creatures are said to be consubstantial when they belong to the same species, whereas the consubstantiality of the divine persons implies numerical identity of substance.

Thus, according to Athanasius, one man is of the same nature (ὁμοφυής) and of the same substance (ὁμοούσιος) as another, but a man and a dog are different from each other both in nature and in substance (ἑτεροφυής, ἑτεροούσιος).[2]

Now, one whose philosophical position is that of naive realism would say that one man is consubstantial with another because the matter of one is derived from the matter of the other. But if one has advanced beyond naive realism, at least to a dogmatic realism, one will attend not to what is sensible, but to what is truly affirmed; therefore one will say that one man is consubstantial with another because of each of them the same substantial attributes are truly affirmed.

The theological ambiguity will clearly appear if we compare Peter and Paul, on the one hand, and on the other, the Father

---

1 Etymologically, οὐσία, ὁμός; cf. ἄμα.

2 Athan., *De synodis*, 53; MG 26, 788 C; AW II, 276, 27 ff.

and the Son. Peter and Paul are consubstantial; the Father and the Son are consubstantial. But Peter and Paul are consubstantial, not because they have numerically the same individual substance —for indeed they have not—but because the individual substance of Peter and the really distinct individual substance of Paul both belong to the same species: Peter and Paul are two particular instances of the species, man. The Father and the Son are also consubstantial, but the analogy with Peter and Paul breaks down because unlike the consubstantial Peter and Paul, who are two men, the consubstantial Father and Son are one and the same God: there is numerically only the one God, who is, nonetheless, truly Father and truly Son.

2. So much for the conceptual ambiguity. But how did different authors actually conceive consubstantiality? That is the historical question that we now must tackle. First we shall indicate some very clear and gross oppositions; then we shall make some comments on the council of Nicea; and finally we shall discuss the actual development of the concept of consubstantiality.

3. According to G. Prestige, "The original signification of homoousios, apart from all theological technicality, is simply 'made of the same stuff'. 'Stuff' hear bears a generic sense necessarily, since no objects of physical experience are composed of identical portions of matter".[3] Having provided abundant illustration of this thesis from the writings of the Gnostics and from the writings of Christians (those concerned with secular matters as well as those that are theological), Prestige says:

> "We may therefore conclude that, down to the Council of Nicaea, homoousios was understood in one sense, and in one sense only, namely 'of one stuff' or 'substance'; and that, when it was applied to the divine Persons, it conveyed a metaphor drawn from material objects, just as Paul of Samosata alleged; with, however, that reservation imposed on the application of physical metaphors to the divine nature, which is claimed by Athanasius and Basil . . . in order to safeguard the unity of God". [4]

[3] G. Prestige, *God in Patristic Thought*, London, 1936, p. 197.
[4] *Ibid.*, p. 209.

Prestige's assessment of the situation is accurate at least to this extent, that the materialistic understanding of *homoousios* was so widespread that (1) five bishops, for this very reason, chose to go into exile, rather than subscribe to the formula of Nicea,[5] (2) Eusebius of Caesarea took great care to explain to his flock that the Nicene formula was not to be understood in a materialistic sense,[6] (3) Athanasius,[7] Hilary,[8] and Basil[9] made a point of explicitly ruling out any such interpretation.

4. One may ask, however, whether, when we exclude every materialistic interpretation of the definition "of the same stuff", we are left with even a metaphor. For the naive realist this is a genuine difficulty; for he thinks of the real in terms of what is presented to the senses. It is not a difficulty for the critical realist, or for one who is at least a dogmatic realist; for the dogmatic and the critical realist think of the real, not as what is sensible, but as what is known through true judgment.

To explain what this means, we may begin with an illustration from a period much later than that at present under discussion. The Latin liturgy, in its preface for Trinity Sunday, says: "For what from your revelation we believe about your glory, that without difference or distinction we hold about your Son and about the Holy Spirit".

Now, what we believe to be revealed about the glory of the Father is not that the Father is some divine "stuff". What in fact we believe to be revealed is the truth about the Father, which has been communicated to us by his true Word; and it is what is *true* of the Father that is to be acknowledged as *true* also of the Son and the Holy Spirit, without any difference or diminution.

The trinitarian Preface, however, does not explain that the

[5] Cf. above, p. 73.
[6] Cf. above, p. 75.
[7] Cf. below, pp. 99 f.
[8] Hilar., *De synodis*, 67 ff; ML 10, 525 ff.
[9] Basil, *Epist.*, 52, 1; MG 32, 393 A.

meaning of the term, *homoousion*, is to be expressed by a circumlocution; such an explanation we find in Basil, who writes:

> "Therefore, if we want to define the essence of two or more things which have the same kind of existence, we do not assign to each of them a separate definition. For example, the words we use to express the essence of Paul will also serve for Timothy, and for Silvanus; and these three are consubstantial, because they share the same essential definition".[10]

Athanasius expresses the same doctrine more concretely, when he says that what is said of the Father is also to be said of the Son, except that the Son is Son, and not Father. Having laid down this rule, Athanasius goes on at once to offer as proof for it that the titles, "God", "the Omnipotent", "the Lord", "the Light", "Who takes away sins" are applied in the scriptures to the Son as well as the Father; and from John 16, 5; 17, 10, he infers that what is true of these particular titles is true of all others too.[11] Alexander of Alexandria was ahead of Athanasius in teaching this doctrine: before the council of Nicea he had affirmed that "the Son is less than the Father only in this, that he is not unbegotten",[12] and he ruled out every element of materialism in the manner of understanding how the Father generated the Son.[13]

[10] Basil, *Epist.*, 38, 2; MG 32, 325 C. Elsewhere, however, Basil considers inadequate the explanation of consubstantiality that he himself gives here: "For, contrary to what some think, things that are related to each other as brothers are not termed consubstantial; but when a cause and what has existence from that cause are both of the same nature they are termed consubstantial." *Epist.*, 52, 2; MG 32, 395 C. This can be understood in two ways. Either Basil defined consubstantiality by a correct twofold reference; if one thing has its origin from another, and if both share the same essential definition, they are consubstantial; or else, failing to get away completely from a material notion, he thought that a relation of origin was of the essence of consubstantiality. We have no need to investigate the mind of Basil here, but as an indication one might take the following: ". . . but now I say that substance means material substrate (*subjectum*). . . ." *Adv. Eunom.*, II, 4; MG 29, 577 C.

[11] Athan., *Orat. 3 c. Arian.*, 4; MG 26, 329 B; cited below, p. 101.

[12] Alex., *Ad Alex. ep. Thess.*, AW III, 27, 14 f.

[13] *Ibid.*, 1, 5 f.

5. If the philosophical ambiguity of the term, *homoousion*, arises from the fact that some take οὐσία to mean body, or matter,[14] whereas others take it to mean that which is, that which is truly affirmed to be, the theological ambiguity, as we have remarked, is rooted in the real difference between the consubstantiality of the divine persons, on the one hand, and that of creatures, on the other. For the consubstantiality of the divine persons means that they have numerically the same substance, whereas consubstantiality in the realm of creation implies numerically distinct individual substances that are specifically the same.

One very familiar illustration of this theological ambiguity is the doctrine of Apollinaris, who denied that Christ had a human soul; therefore, according to him, the incarnate Word, as incarnate, is not consubstantial with us.[15] The orthodox position, on the other hand, as expressed both in the Formula of Union (DS 272) and in the decree of Chalcedon (DS 301 f), is that the Son is consubstantial with the Father in respect of his deity, and consubstantial with us in respect of his humanity. Indeed, even the Severian Monophysites, who would allow no distinction whatever between hypostasis and nature, professed, of their own accord, this dual consubstantiality of the Son: with the Father in respect of his deity, and with us in respect of his humanity.[16] In this whole discussion, however, the term *homoousion* is taken in a twofold sense, since the human substance of Christ, and that of Peter, and that of Paul, are numerically distinct from each other, whereas the divine substance of the Father and the Son is numerically one and the same.

Underlying this ambiguity is the divine mystery itself: for we do not grasp by the power of our intellects, but believe by faith, that the substance of the Father and that of the Son is one and

[14] Several examples in Orbe, *Primera teología*, p. 677, n. 11; for further examples see *ibid.*, index, s.v. οὐσία.

[15] H. Lietzmann, *Apollinaris von Laodicaea*, Tübingen, 1904, pp. 213, 19 and 214, 23.

[16] J. Lebon, in Grillmeier-Bacht, *Das Konzil von Chalkedon*, Würzburg, 1951, I, 435 and 438 f.

the same substance. For this reason, it is only those who believe in the Trinity, and then only by dint of clear and consistent reasoning, who can overcome every difficulty. Others, however, go off in different directions, to end up in diametrically opposed positions: *homoousion*, as applied to the divine Persons, is taken to mean (1) that there is no real distinction between the Father and the Son, and (2) that the Father and the Son are not only two distinct persons, but also two gods. For if one starts out with a materialistic understanding of consubstantiality and then, ruling out every materialistic connotation of the term, applies it to the divine persons, since it is matter that grounds the distinction between corporeal beings, the denial of matter in God can be taken to imply the negation of all distinction; and so, quite naturally, one will conclude that the term, *homoousion*, as applied to God, smacks of Sabellianism. If, on the other hand, one begins with an understanding of *homoousion* that is derived from attending to true judgment, so that in calling things consubstantial one means that they have the same essential or substantial definition, then, since in the world of our experience, there are as many human substances as there are human persons, one may be led to infer, by parity of reasoning, that since there are three divine persons, or hypostases, so there are also three gods; and so, again quite naturally, and again quite falsely, the term *homoousion* will be considered suspect, but now because it seems to imply a tritheism.

6. It seems, in fact, that in the earlier phase of Arianism, the opponents of the council of Nicea were unwilling even to utter the word, *homoousion*. For example, if we may go by the index appended by E. Klostermann to his edition of Eusebius of Caesarea's *Against Marcellus* and *On Ecclesiastical Theology*, in neither of these works does the word *homoousion* occur at all— neither as used by Eusebius himself, nor within the passages that he cites from Marcellus.[17] Again, if we look at the multiplicity of creeds that emerged from the various minor councils between

[17] E. Klostermann, *Eusebius Werke* (GCS 14), Leipzig, 1906.

the years 340 and 360, we might almost say that the only difference between them is this, that whereas the earlier ones make no
mention at all of the term *homoousion*, a number of the later ones
explicitly exclude it.[18]

At that stage of the dispute, the main burden of the attack on
homoousion would appear to have been that it favoured Sabellianism. For this was the charge brought against Marcellus of
Ancyra, both by Eusebius and by the minor councils. Yet
Marcellus took part in the council of Nicea and later, together
with Athanasius, with whom he had taken refuge in Rome, he
had been pronounced guiltless and readmitted to communion[19]
(Athanasius dissociated himself from Marcellus only when the
Ebionite christology appeared clearly in Marcellus' disciple,
Photinus). Clearer evidence of the same point is provided by
the doctrine of the Homoeousians, whose only quarrel, in the
judgment of Athanasius, was with the word, *homoousion*.[20] They
certainly understood the word in a Sabellian sense, since they
condemned ὁμοούσιον and ταὐτοούσιον alike[21], asserted that there
were three hypostases, but not three gods,[22] and taught that the
Son is similar to the Father in respect of his substance,[23] as in
every other respect.[24]

In the later period, when the Cappadocians were engaged in
refuting the Eunomians, the twofold charge of Sabellianism,
and tritheism alike, was levelled against the *homoousion*.[25] Since
that, however, is an internally inconsistent position, the liberal
theologians accused the Cappadocians only of tritheism, of
which they also accused even Athanasius himself.[26]

[18] See Hahn, pp. 183–216; cf. above, p. 83.

[19] Cf. P. Smulders, *La doctrine trinitaire de saint Hilaire*, pp. 21 ff, 29.

[20] Athan., *De synodis*, 41; AW II, 266 f; MG 26, 765 A.

[21] Epiphan., *Haer.*, 73, 11, 10; Holl III, 284, 5.

[22] *Ibid.*, 73, 16; Holl, 288, 20 ff.

[23] *Ibid.*, 73, 13; Holl, 285, 29 ff.

[24] *Ibid.*, 73, 12; Holl, 284, 12 ff.

[25] Cf. Basil, *Epist.*, 189, 2; MG 32, 686 B.

[26] [Lonergan here gives a reference to a later, untranslated part of the book.
Trans.]

7. In interpreting the decree of the council of Nicea one must distinguish between its explicit and its implicit content; with regard to its implicit content one must make a further distinction, between a merely logical implication, on the one hand, and on the other, a conclusion that was actually drawn.

Now, the council of Nicea set itself in direct opposition to those who asserted that the Son was not God, but a creature. Explicitly, therefore, it affirmed its faith in one God, adding at once, the Father almighty; then it named the Son, calling him Lord, God of God, begotten, not made, of the Father's substance, and consubstantial with the Father (DS 125). However, the decree of the council does not teach, in so many words, that the substance of the Father and that of the Son is one and the same substance.

Still, the affirmation of a single substance is logically contained in the Nicene decree. For *in the first place*, the council Fathers were monotheists. But if there is only one God, and the Father is truly God, and the Son is also truly God, then it follows necessarily that the divinity of the Father, and that of the Son, is one and the same divinity. *Secondly*, according to Athanasius, the council Fathers at first thought of writing that the Son is the true image of the Father, in every way most like the Father, but then, having seen how the Arians could get around such phrases

"they were forced, first, to go back again to the scriptures, to establish their position, and then to state more unambiguously what they had stated before, and finally, to write that the Son is consubstantial with the Father, in order to signify that the Son is not just similar to the Father, but is the same thing in similitude out of the Father. . . .".[27]

Athanasius thus testifies to the fact that the Nicene decree is intended to go beyond the affirmation of a mere similarity between the Father and the Son, to an affirmation of identity.

However, where and when the identity in substance of the Father and the Son, which is logically implied by the Nicene decree, was actually deduced as a logical conclusion, can be

[27] Athan., *De decretis nic. syn.*, 20; MG 25, 452 B; AW II, 17, 7–10.

settled only by historical investigation. Certainly present in the council of Sardica, in 343, where it is taught that the hypostasis of the Father and that of the Son are one and the same hypostasis,[28] it would not appear to be present, a few years before the council of Nicea, in the letter of Alexander of Alexandria, which speaks of the Father and the Son as "two natures in hypostasis".[29] And Athanasius' own expression, "the same thing in similitude", which we cited above, suggests that it took some time for a satisfactory formulation of the doctrine to be worked out.[30]

8. Our final task in this section will be to discuss the actual development of the notion of consubstantiality, from the initial meaning of "being of the same stuff" to the dogmatic and theological meaning that it came eventually to convey.

Since the scriptures call the Son "the effulgence of his glory and the stamp of his very being" (Heb 1, 3), "the image of God" (2 Cor 4, 4; Col 1, 15) and "the wisdom of God" (1 Cor 1, 24), it is not surprising that the ancient Christian authors also applied to the Son what they found in the book of Wisdom: ".... the vapor of God's power, a pure and unadulterated emanation of the effulgence of the omnipotent God ... the brightness of the eternal light, the spotless mirror of God's majesty and the image of his goodness" (Wis 7, 25). Neither are they to be blamed for adding other images, saying that the Son proceeds from the

---

[28] Cf. Hahn, pp. 188 ff. Or in Theodoret, HE II, 6; MG 82, 1012 CD. Note that Athanasius expressly affirmed that this formula was neither approved nor promulgated by the council of Sardica, *Tom ad Antioch.*, 5; MG 26, 799 C.

[29] Alex., *Epist. ad Alex. ep. Thess.*, IX; MG 18, 561 B; AW III, 25, 23. This expression of Alexander's is aimed directly against Sabellianism.

[30] Clear intention is not matched by exact expression when it is said: ἵνα μὴ μόνον ὅμοιον τὸν υἱόν, ἀλλὰ ταὐτὸν τῇ ὁμοιώσει ἐκ τοῦ πατρὸς εἶναι σημαίνωσι..., *De decretis nic. syn.*, 20; cf. above, n. 27. Here there is a clear denial of mere similarity and a clear affirmation of a certain identity; but there is some obscurity about the identity that is "in similitude out of the Father". Compare what Athanasius says elsewhere: "For though the Son, as being begotten, is something different, as being God he is the same." *Orat. 3 c. Arian.*, 4; MG 26, 328 C.

Father as offspring from parent, stream from source, brightness from the sun, light from light, fire from fire, or as one torch from another.[31]

Our interest, however, is not in the images themselves, but in what was grasped in the images, namely, the notion of consubstantiality. We do not mean the notion of consubstantiality as it was later expounded systematically, but as it was grasped, at that time, by insight into the data of sense and of imagination. For there is, in every science, an early stage, in which insight grasps in data the form, or intrinsic intelligibility, of things, and a later stage, in which that insight receives adequate expression.

As a first illustration we may take the reasoning of Dionysius of Alexandria (died 264–265), who, while admitting that he did not use the word consubstantial, insisted nonetheless that he had used other equivalent expressions—meaning the various images to which we have just referred. He writes:

> "For I used the example of human offspring, which, as is obvious, is of the same genus as its progenitor; indeed, I said that the only difference between parents and their children is that the parents are not themselves their children . . . I said that a plant, which grows from seed or root, is different from that from which it sprouts, although it is of exactly the same nature; that the stream that flows from the source has another name and another form, for we do not say that the stream is the source, or that the source is the stream; yet both of them exist, and the source is, as it were, the father, and the stream is water flowing from the source . . . But in the third book he says: The life was begotten of life, as a river coming from its source, or as a brilliant light, lit from light inextinguishable".[32]

If the reasoning of Dionysius—or of Athanasius, who reports him—is valid, then it amounts to the same thing to employ these images or to pronounce the word, consubstantial.

---

[31] Cf. F. J. Dölger, "Sonne und Sonnenstrahl als Gleichnis in der Logos-theologie des christlichen Altertums", *Antike und Christentum*, I (1929), 271–290; I. Ortiz de Urbina, *El simbolo Niceno*, Madrid, 1947, pp. 140 ff; A. Orbe, *Primera teología*, pp. 38–57 and *passim*.

[32] Athan., *De sententia Dionysii*, 18; MG 25, 505 B–508 A; cf. *De decretis nic. syn.*, 25; MG 25, 461 BC; *De synodis*, 44; MG 26, 769 BC; AW II, 59, 21, 269.

In the support of the contention that the images in question and the notion of consubstantiality are intimately connected, Athanasius could have adduced, from the *Apology for Origen* of St. Pamphilus the martyr, what Pamphilus attributes to Origen himself:

"He uses the word, vapor, taking an image from corporeal things, but this he does in order that we might gain some slight understanding of the manner in which Christ, who is the wisdom of God, comes out of God. Thus, like the vapor that arises from some corporeal substance, so he arises as a kind of vapor from the power of God himself; wisdom, proceeding thus from God, is generated of God's own substance. Again taking an image from corporeal things, he says that he is a pure and unadulterated emanation of the glory of the almighty. Both of these metaphors show most clearly that the Son is of the same substance as the Father. For is an emanation not homoousios, that is, of one substance with the body of which it is an emanation or vapor?"[33]

If it is true that the metaphors of vapor and emanation "show most clearly" that the Son is of the same substance as the Father, it is no surprise to learn that Theognostus, who was for some years head of the exegetical school at Alexandria, reasoned as follows, in the second volume of his work, *Hypotyposeis,*

"The substance of the Son was not made from something outside of the Father, nor was it made from nothing; it was born of the Father's substance, as brightness is born of light and vapor of water. For the brightness of the sun is not the sun itself, nor is the vapor the water itself. Neither, on the other hand, is the Son's substance something foreign to the Father; for it emanates from the Father's own substance—in such a way, however, that the Father's own substance is not in any way divided. For as the sun, ever remaining the same, is in no way diminished by the emanation of its rays, so the Father's substance undergoes no change, when he has the Son as his own image".[34]

---

[33] MG 14, 1308 CD. Prestige (*op. cit.*, p. 200) attributes this scholion on the epistle to the Hebrews to Origen himself. As far as our present discussion is concerned, it matters little whether it is from Origen himself, or from some other author more ancient than Pamphilus.

[34] Athan., *De decretis nic. syn.*, 25; MG 25, 459 C; AW II, 21, 1-7.

The manner of conceiving the relationship between the Father and the Son, which we found in the older authors, we find also in Athanasius himself, who argued as follows:

"How can you aptly describe how the brightness is related to the light, or the stream to the source, or the Son to the Father, except by using the word, consubstantial?"[35]

".... thus, to be offspring, and to be consubstantial, mean one and the same thing; and whoever thinks of the Son as the offspring (gennêma) of the Father, rightly holds that he is consubstantial with the Father."[36]

"But then the bishops, seeing through the deceits of the Arians, went to the scriptures and there collected these words: brightness, source, stream and the figure of his substance. They also adduced the phrases, 'In your light we shall see the light' and 'I and the Father are one'. Then, concisely and more clearly, they wrote that the Son is consubstantial with the Father; for that is what the other phrases all mean".[37]

According to Athanasius, therefore, the very familiar comparisons contain within them the meaning of consubstantiality, provided that one takes care to exclude any imperfection that is attendant on being corporeal and being created:

"For as regards bodies that are similar to each other, they can certainly be far away from each other, as children are often far away from their parents ... But the Son is begotten of the Father in a manner altogether different from that of human generation; not only is he similar to the Father's substance, but he cannot be divided from it; for he and the Father are one, and the Word is always in the Father, and the Father in the Word; so the Son is related to the Father as its brightness is related to the sun—for the comparison carries this meaning. Therefore the synod (of Nicea), rightly understanding the matter, wrote that the Son is consubstantial with the Father, in order to overthrow the perversity of the heretics, and to show that the Word is different from all things that have been made".[38]

It is clear enough, then, how Athanasius' own mind worked, and, at least by his account, also the minds of the ante-Nicene

[35] Athan., *De synodis*, 41; MG 26, 765 C; AW II, 267, 18 f.
[36] *Ibid.*, 42; MG 26, 768 C; AW II, 268, 13 f.
[37] Athan., *Ad afros.*, 6; MG 26, 1040 AB.
[38] Athan., *De decretis nic. syn.*, 20; MG 25, 452 C; AW II, 17, 12–21.

authors and of the council Fathers at Nicea. They began with the images, taken mostly from scripture, with which we are now so familiar; in these images they grasped a certain intelligibility, which they expressed in the concept of consubstantiality; then, taking this concept of consubstantiality, derived from what is sensible, they adapted it, mainly in accordance with sayings of scripture itself, to the best of their ability, in order to conceive the divine generation of the Son.

Athanasius certainly insisted on the need for the final step of adaptation: as the meaning of the word, Son, had to be adapted, so too had the meaning of the word, consubstantial:

> "When we speak of him as offspring, we do not understand this in a human way, and when we acknowledge God as Father, we do not attribute bodily characteristics to him: these words and images we apply to God in a fitting manner, for God is not like man. In the same way, when we hear him described as consubstantial, we must transcend the senses utterly and, following the Proverb (23, 1), understand spiritually what is laid before us, to know that as life comes from the source and brightness from the light, so he is truly Son, out of the Father, and like the Father".[39]

As an indication of the extent to which Athanasius himself achieved this adaptation and purification we may cite the following:

> ' . . . therefore, let us not say that there are two gods, but only one, since there is only one divinity, just as there is only the one form, both of the light and of its brightness. And that is what appeared to Jacob: the scripture says, 'The sun rose upon him, after the form of God had passed' (Gen 27,31). When the holy prophets saw this, and understood whose Son and image he was they said, 'The word of the Lord came to me' (Is 38,4; Jer 1,2; 4,11); and when they recognized that the Father was seen and revealed in him, they confidently asserted, 'The God of our fathers appeared to me, the God of Abraham, and of Isaac, and of Jacob (Ex 3,16)'. Since that is so, why are we afraid to say that he is consubstantial with the Father, and shows us what the Father is like—he who is like the Father, and one in divinity with him? For if, as has often been said, he, as Son, is not similar to

[39] Athan., De synodis, 42; MG 26, 768 AB; AW II, 267, 27 ff.

and has no share in the Father's substance, then, of course, we are right to avoid using the word. If, on the other hand, he is the Father's own illuminating and creative power, without which the Father neither creates nor is known (for through him, and in him, all things are held together), why do we refuse to use the word that expresses this understanding of him? What else does it mean, to be of the same nature as the Father, if not, to be consubstantial with him? For it is not as if God, needing somebody to help him, assumed a son from outside of himself; neither are the things that God made equal to him in dignity, so that they ought to be honoured as he is honoured, or that we should say that they and the Father are one. Besides, who will say that the sun and its brightness are two different lights, or different substances? Or who will say that the brightness of the sun is an accident of the sun, and not purely and simply the sun's offspring, in such manner that, while the sun and its brightness are two things, they are nonetheless the one light, because the brightness comes from the sun? Since the nature of the Son is even more inseparable from the Father than the brightness of the sun is from the sun itself, and since the divinity of the Son is not something added to him—but the divinity of the Father is in the Son, so that whoever sees the Son sees the Father in him—why should the Son, who is like this, not be called consubstantial with the Father"?[40]

"Thus, the Son is not another god, because he is not something from outside of God. If one were to think of any divinity outside of God, then one would be introducing several gods. For although the Son, as begotten, is other than the Father, still, as God he is the same as the Father; and so he and the Father are one, both as having the same nature and as sharing the same divinity, as we have said. For the brightness itself is also light; it does not come after the sun, nor is it another light, nor does it become light by participating in the sun's light, but it is, in the fullest sense, the sun's offspring. Where light, in this way, gives birth to light, there is, of necessity, only one light, and it cannot be said that the sun and its brightness are two different lights; the sun and its brightness are two things, but there is one light, born of the sun, which with its brightness illuminates the whole universe. Similarly, the Son's divinity is also that of the Father, and so there is but the one divinity; so also there is but one God, and no other God apart from him. Therefore, because they are one, and because the divinity itself is also one, what is said of the Father is also said of the Son, except the name, Father. Thus, therefore, the Son is called God: *And the Word was God*; he is also called the Omnipotent: *Thus says the Omnipotent, who was,*

[40] Athan., *De synodis*, 52; MG 26, 785 C–788 B; AW II, 275, 34 ff.

and who is, and who is to come; similarly, he is the Lord: *The one Lord, Jesus Christ*; and he is also called the Light: *I am the Light*; and further, he is said to take away sins: *But that you may know*, he says, *that the Son of Man on earth has power to forgive sins*; and there are many other similar sayings in scripture. For the Son himself says: *All things that the Father has are mine*; and again: *What I have is yours*".[41]

There are four things to be noted in these passages: (1) an initial notion of consubstantiality, grasped in created things, and expressed through a combination of the concepts of originating-from, being-similar-to, and being-conjoined-to; (2) the principles that must guide the ascent from created things, presented to the senses, to some conception of the triune God; (3) the interpretation of the original image in the light of these principles; and (4) the terminal notion of consubstantiality, as applied to the Trinity.

The initial notion is attached to various images, but the most common image is that of the sun and its brightness. For the brightness has its origin in the sun, and indeed, it is of the very nature of the sun to give forth its brightness, and of the brightness to go forth from the sun. The brightness of the sun is most like the sun, and is, in fact, the sun itself in its appearing. There is the closest possible union between the sun and its brightness: so close that neither one could be without the other; so close that it is one and the same light that is in the sun and in its brightness.

Secondly, the principles that must guide the ascent from the things of sense to a conception of the Trinity are known only in part by the natural light of reason; in part they can be known only by divine revelation. For the light of natural reason can do no more than conclude to the fact of God's existence, and work out some analogous concept of God (DS 3026); natural reason can neither understand nor demonstrate the mystery of the Blessed Trinity (DS 3041).

Thirdly, the interpretation of the original image in the light

[41] Athan., *Orat.* 3 *c. Arian.*, 4; MG 26, 328 C–329 B; The texts cited are: Jn. 1, 1; Rev. 1, 8; 1 Cor. 8, 6; Jn. 8, 12; Lk. 5, 24; Jn. 16, 15; 17, 10.

of these principles will depend on both the intelligence and the diligence that is applied to the complex task of (1) avoiding metaphors and anthropomorphisms, (2) selecting appropriate aspects of created things from which, by analogy, one can ascend to some conception of God, and (3) attending to and applying the words of sacred scripture, through which alone the mystery of the Trinity is made known to us.

Thus, in the passages cited above, Athanasius interpreted the image in this way: It is one and the same light that is in the sun and in its brightness; in some way corresponding to this one light, there is the one manifestation or aspect of the divinity, which is the Word of God, the image of God the Father, the Father's own power of illumination and creation, and the divinity of the Father in the Son, revealed to the prophets of old and attested by them, revealed and attested at last by the Son himself, who says: Whoever sees me, also sees the Father (John 14, 9).

Finally, the terminal notion of consubstantiality not only transcends every image, but also somehow transcends every intelligibility grasped in an image. For just as Maxwell's equations for the electro-magnetic field emerged, in the first place, from images, but have themselves no corresponding image, so the rule of Athanasius refers not to images, but only to concepts and to judgments. What the rule states is that what is said of the Father is also to be said of the Son, except that the Son is Son and not Father. Not only does this rule prescind from all images; there is nothing imaginable in which it can be grasped or understood.

The rule of Athanasius became a commonplace in later theology, but it appears differently there than it does in the writings of Athanasius himself. In later writings it is given a systematic grounding and a technical expression: in God there is the one *ousia*, the one divinity, the one power and the one operation, but there are three divine persons, who are really distinct from each other, distinguished from each other by their personal properties of relationship; and everything that belongs to the three divine persons is one, except where there is the opposition of reciprocal relationship.[42] In Athanasius, however, the rule is more like the final conclusion towards which, more or less directly, the whole of his work is heading. And so, if one can only understand what is static, what does not change and develop, one will have little understanding of much that Athanasius had to say. Take, for example, the phrase that we cited above, in which he says that the Son is not only similar to the Father but is "the same thing in similitude out of the Father".[43] Here Athanasius denies that there is merely a similarity between the Father and the Son, and affirms a certain identity between them. But one will hardly make much sense of this identity-in-similitude if, prescinding from the whole genetic process from the images to the terminal notion of consubstantiality, one considers only the rule concerning the divine attributes.

But besides, Athanasius did not make use of the distinction drawn later between *ousia* and *hypostasis*. Though he knew of this distinction and understood it,[44] he himself judged that οὐσία, τὸ ὄν, ὕπαρξις and ὑπόστασις all meant and said the same thing.[45]

[42] [Lonergan here refers to the third thesis in the second part of this volume Trans.]

[43] Athan., *De decretis nic. syn.*, 20; MG 25, 452 B; Opitz, AW II, 17, 9. Cf. C. Hauret, *Comment le 'Defenseur de Nicée' a-t-il compris le dogme de Nicée*, Bruges, 1936; J. Lebon, *Rev. d'hist. eccl.*, 47 (1952), 485–529.

[44] Athan., *Tom. ad Antioch.*, 5; MG 26, 801 AB

[45] Athan., *Epist. ad Afros*, 4; MG 26, 1036 B.

SECTION X

THE STRUCTURE OF THE ANTE-NICENE MOVEMENT

1. It should now be sufficiently clear that there are certain prerequisites to the proper use of the ante-Nicene Christian authors as witnesses to the doctrine of the Blessed Trinity. For unless one has thoroughly understood all that we related above about "homoousion", "of one substance", "the image of goodness itself", Arianism and semi-Arianism, Sabellianism, Gnosticism and Judaeo-Christianity, two things will happen: first, what the ante-Nicene authors actually said will seem very strange indeed, and second, from what they failed to say one will draw false conclusions about what they held.

Yet however necessary all of this is, it is not yet sufficient. The abundance and variety of the material, unless it be drawn together in a manner that displays a pattern or order, are more likely to obfuscate than to illuminate the mind, to cloud the issue rather than clarify it.

Our quest for order and clarity would be much less exacting, of course, if the development of trinitarian doctrine had taken place in some sort of cultural and doctrinal vacuum. In fact, however, it was very much tied in with other movements, having to do with scriptural exegesis, the influence of Stoic and Platonic philosophy, and the very manner of conceiving God. Nor is that all. For these movements are as the waves that rise up on the surface of a storm-tossed sea; below them is a deeper and more powerful current, namely, the drive towards drawing together the whole heritage of the Hebrews and of the Greeks, to form a new, Christian mode of thought and style of life.

Beginning, then, from what is more fundamental, we shall first present some schemes or patterns of culture and cultural development in general [§ 2], and of the difference between the culture of the Hebrews and that of the Greeks, in particular [§ 3]; next we shall sketch the development of scriptural exegesis [§ 4], of the influence of Greek philosophy [§ 5], and of the Christian conception of God [§ 6]; finally, coming to our own particular topic, we shall attempt an outline of the development of trinitarian theology [§ 7].

2. *Culture and cultural development*

There are two quite different views of culture. There is an older, classicist, normative view, according to which one draws a distinction between the cultured and the uncultured. But there is also a modern view, which is empirical and anthropological: it acknowledges a multiplicity of cultures, so that the lowliest and the most primitive of tribes have a culture, no less than the most advanced and highly-developed peoples. It is the latter, empirical view of culture that we adopt here.

What we might call the material element of culture is made up of human capacities, human dispositions and habits, and human operations and their products. Capacities, dispositions and habits, operations and products are all interrelated: dispositions and habits are perfections and determinations of capacities; operations proceed promptly, spontaneously and with ease from dispositions and habits; and products, finally, are the results of operations.

Next, we must note a certain principle or law of combination and composition. For operations are such that they can be joined one to another, to yield a composite product; indeed, a certain few basic operations, taken in a great variety of permutations and combinations, can yield an enormous diversity of results. So, for example, once one has learnt how to write the comparatively few letters contained in the alphabet of any language, one has the necessary equipment for writing everything that is said in that language. The same principle applies to the other arts, whether liberal or practical: in all of these some basic operations are discovered, which can then be modified, in various measures and to varying degrees, and adapted to new circumstances, and so there arises the possibility of an immense range of permutations and combinations. And the same applies to the sciences. If, for example, one examines the geometry of Euclid, or the *Contra Gentiles* of St. Thomas, one will find that the separate theorems or conclusions proceed from a relatively small number of operations, differently modified and adapted to suit different circumstances. Finally, it is not, of course, only the operations of separate individuals that can combine in this way; every instance of whatever kind of human collaboration involves the combination of operations of different individuals, to yield a composite product.

But the reason why we act, or operate, is in order to attain some good. Since our ultimate end is essential goodness, our proximate ends are good by participation, and they are of three kinds: particular goods, the good of order, and value. Particular goods are all those things that meet the needs of particular individuals in particular places at particular times. The good of order is a formal principle that ensures a continual flow of particular goods; for example, matrimonial systems, technological, economical and political systems, literary and scientific systems, educational and religious systems are all goods of order. The good of value, finally, is what inspires a rational choice between one good of order and another, for example, Christian marriage, capitalism, democracy, etc.

One might infer from all of this that what happens is that different races, having different scales of value, choose different goods of order, so that they may enjoy a steady flow of such and such particular goods, arising from such and such particular operations. That, however, would be a somewhat abstract, atemporal way of viewing human affairs. Concretely, values are perceived only in the good of order itself, the good of order is perceived only in the particular goods that it ensures, and the only actual particular goods are those that men, by the operations that they have in fact carried out, have learnt how to produce or to acquire. And so, if one wants to understand how cultures emerge and develop, it is rather on the operations that one ought to focus, to discover how they are carried out, how they are combined with each other, how they gradually coalesce into larger complexes, until eventually a kind of dynamic structure emerges—a structure, however, which is, as it were, only implicitly informed by the good of order and actuated by value, its proximate manifestation being men and women, united in friendship or divided by discord, carrying out operations that are aimed at the attainment of particular goods.

Let us move on rapidly now to the point that we want to make, which is that some cultures remain for centuries almost unchanged, while others, whether from some kind of internal tension or from the pressure of external circumstances, keep finding new modes of operation, introducing new modifications of operations, trying out new permutations and combinations and enjoying new particular goods, and so even come to experiment with the good of order itself and to perceive new human values. To this fundamental kind of cultural evolution another kind is added when, by the process of communication or by the intermingling of peoples, two different cultures flow into and unite with each other, each adapting to the other, so that a third culture emerges, which is a kind of composite of the other two.

3. *The differences between Hebrew culture and Greek culture*

Going back, first, beyond all the differences between the Hebrews and the Greeks, and back beyond every difference between any one culture and any other, to what is at the root of all cultures, we recall B. Malinowski's[1] contention, that primitives display no less intelligence and reasonableness than anybody else, as long as they are involved in the practical tasks of daily living; that it is only when they move outside the famil-

[1] B. Malinowski, *Magic, Science and Religion*, New York, 1954 [Doubleday Anchor Book, A 23]. R. Redfield, *The Primitive World and its Transformations*, Ithaca, N.Y., 1959[1]. H. Frankfort and others, *Before Philosophy*, Penguin 1959[5].

iar sphere of immediate experience that myth and magic invade, envelop and dominate everything.

But if we leave the primitive aside, and move on to the ancient high civilisations of Egypt, Mesopotamia and Crete, of the valleys of the Indus and the Hoang Ho, or, on the American continent, of the Incas, the Mayas and the Toltecs, we find that while the external circumstances are vastly different from those of the primitives, the basic pattern is more or less the same. The area over which man exercises his practical intelligence has increased enormously: all the arts of construction, of writing, of calculating, and of organisation, are being impressively cultivated; yet political and religious life is still dominated by myth and magic. According to K. Jaspers there came a turning-point, a kind of axial period, between the years 800 and 200 B.C., when, with the destruction of the great, stable empires, men were more or less forced to develop their individual use of reason, and, accepting their responsibility as persons, undermined the power of myth.[2]

There were, however, notable differences in the manner in which this development took place. It was through literature, philosophy and science that the Greeks achieved the differentiation of consciousness that created the world of theory, which then directed and controlled the everyday world of practical common sense. One might say, then, that the Greeks drew out and developed from natural human capacities the instrument that of its very nature is opposed to myth and magic. The Hebrews, however, took quite a different route. They did not undermine myth by theory but, schooled by divine revelation, they broke its power, while remaining within the common sense world of practical living and retaining its categories. For they conceived God as a person, whom they identified with and recognised in certain concrete events: it was God who, in the Patriarchs and in Moses, and through the prophets, performed such and such deeds, said such and such, gave such and such

[2] K. Jaspers, *The Origin and Goal of History*, Trans. Bullock, London, Routledge, 1953.

commands, made such and such promises and issued such and such threats to the people. In conceiving God in this way, the Hebrews did not manage to avoid all anthropomorphism, nor did they succeed in explaining that what was symbolic was only symbolic; yet they had a truer knowledge of God than did the Greeks, they were more fully liberated from myth, and they had available more efficacious means for living a good life.[3]

Against the background of this twofold development it was almost inevitable that the Christians who lived under the sway of the Roman empire should come to ask themselves how they ought to combine the religion they had received from the Jews with the culture developed by the Greeks.[4]

4. The hermeneutical problem

Although it was quite some time before this problem was formulated in theoretical language, it was present from the early days of the Christian Church. For those who were using both the Hebrew Old Testament and the Greek New Testament could hardly avoid having difficulties of understanding and interpretation. Then, with the multiplication of the apocryphal writings, there was need to determine the canon of scripture; and with the rise and spread of heresies the very complexity of the problem gradually brought it about that the Alexandrians saw fit to publish an authentic text of the scriptures, to establish principles of interpretation and to compose commentaries on the most difficult passages. We must first describe this movement, at least in outline, because there were other movements, of even greater significance, that were carried along by its impetus.

A central problem was the interpretation of symbols. For while symbols are a particularly effective, and indeed necessary, means of penetrating man's sensibility and arousing his affecti-

[3] On this difference between the Hebrews and the Greeks, cf. E. Voegelin, *Order and History*, 3 vol., Louisiana State University Press, 1956, 1957. [A fourth volume appeared in 1974. *Trans.*]

[4] Cf. J. Daniélou, *Gospel Message.* . . .

vity, they are apt to be somewhat ambiguous vehicles of the truth. We have already seen how the Judaeo-Christians, through an interpretation of Isaiah 6, 1 ff, represented the doctrine of the Blessed Trinity symbolically. The Elkesites, however, not only called the Son and the Holy Spirit angels; they also described them as having enormous dimensions, measured in miles and acres, and the Son was male, the Holy Spirit female.[5] We know that other Judaeo-Christians went further, saying that the Son was nothing more than an angel.[6] And some of them, accepting only Jesus' own words, considered Paul not an apostle, but an apostate from the Law.[7]

We have already given some indication of how much trouble the Gnostics caused, but we may add here the following passage from Ireneus:

"They say that these things [the Gnostic system] are not said openly [in the scriptures], since not everybody knows them, but that they have been shown by our Saviour, in a mysterious way, through parables, to those who can understand. Thus, as we have noted before, they say that the thirty Aeons are signified by the thirty years of our Saviour's hidden life, and by the parable of the workers in the vineyard.[8] And they say it is perfectly clear that Paul very frequently refers to the Aeons, even preserving their order, as when he says: 'Through all the generations of the ages' [Eph. 3,21]. We ourselves, according to them, refer to those Aeons when, giving thanks to God, we say, 'the aeons of aeons'. Indeed, wherever there is any mention of an aeon, or of aeons, they would have it that it is a reference to *their* Aeons. They say that the emission of the Dodecad of Aeons is signified by the fact that the Lord, at the age of Twelve, disputed with the doctors

[5] Hippol., *Refutatio*, IX, 13; Wendland (GCS 26), 251, 11 ff; MG 16[3], 3387 BC; cf. J. Daniélou, *The Theology of Jewish Christianity*, p. 140; Orig. *In Joan.*, II, 12; Preuschen, 67, 20.

[6] Epiphan., *Haer.*, 30, 16; Holl I, 354, 4; MG 41, 432.

[7] *Hom. Clem.*, XVI, 15; B. Rehm (GCS 42), 15-18; MG 2, 377 B. Iren., *Adv. Haer.*, I, 26, 2; Harvey, I, 213, where there is an account of the doctrine of the Ebionites.

[8] Iren., *Adv. Haer.*, I, 1, 3; Harvey, I, 12; "For some [workers] are sent about the first hour, some about the third, some about the ninth and some about the eleventh. Now if we add up all the numbers of the hours mentioned here, we get the number thirty".

III

of the Law, and also by the fact that it was twelve apostles that he chose; the remaining eighteen Aeons, they say, are shown by the fact that, after his resurrection from the dead, he remained among his disciples for eighteen months. They also say that the first letters of his name, Iota and Eta, are a further reference to the eighteen Aeons;[9] and the first letter alone, Iota, refers, they say, to the Decad of Aeons. It was for this reason, according to them, that our Saviour said, 'Not one iota and not one point of the law shall pass away, but all shall be accomplished' ".[10]

". . . . It is not only the gospels and the apostolic writings that they use, to try to establish their case, giving false expositions and twisted interpretations; they also appeal to the Law and the Prophets, because there they find many parables and allegories that can be interpreted in many ways. . . .".[11]

However, without going right through the works of Ireneus, one can hardly appreciate just how often he felt called upon to challenge Gnostic exegesis, or at least to make a disparaging reference to it. But if the Christians had just been content to defend themselves against attack, they might have composed massive tomes of refutation, against each of the Gnostic sects in turn, with as little profit from all their efforts as had the barbarian boxer of Demosthenes, who kept moving his hand to protect the spot where he had just been hit; for it is not very hard to discover new heresies or, by taking evasive action, to maintain the old ones.

It is hardly surprising, then, that Clement of Alexandria should have urged a methodical ordering of the questions asked, and then the definition of each of the words used, where the definitions would be clearer than the words they defined, and would be admitted by all. Once a word was defined, one was to determine whether or not any reality corresponded to the word. With that correspondence established one was to inquire into the object's nature and its qualities. Clement then added further notes on proofs, analysis, suppositions, genera and differences, species, categories, causes. All of this was borrowed from the

[9] Where we write 18 or 10 (Roman XVIII or X), the Greeks wrote $\iota\eta'$ or ι'.
[10] Iren., *Adv. Haer.*, I, 3, 1.2; Harvey I, 24-26.
[11] *Ibid.*, I, 3, 6; Harvey I, 31.

Greeks, but Clement had clearly found an effective strategy for the systematic study of scripture, and no less, for withdrawing the minds of men from fruitless symbolic speculations, to direct them towards the true natures of actually existing things.[12]

5. The problem of naive realism

If the remedy for the improper use of symbols was true knowledge of actually existing things, then obviously one had to fix on some determinate notion of reality. We have already referred to the naive realism of Tertullian, who pictured to himself the unity of the divine substance as a kind of organic unity. The difficulty, however, is not Tertullian's alone; it is characteristic of all men, unless and until they become wiser, to suppose, at least implicitly, that the ultimate and basic categories are not those of being, or of substance, but of place and time.

This point can be illustrated from the writings both of Clement of Alexandria and of Ireneus. First we shall take Ireneus, who, wanting to demonstrate that there was only one supreme God, appealed above all to the notions of containing and of being contained:

"For either there must be one who contains all things, who in his own domain made each and every thing that has been made, according to his own will; or else there must be many gods who created, each one of them starting where another ends, each one bordering on another. In the latter case, all the gods must be included in something greater than them all, containing them all; and each one will be confined to his own area; and so none of them can be God. For each one, compared with all the others taken together, will have only a tiny part, and none of them can be called the Omnipotent; and so this view leads necessarily to impiety".[13]

Then, as if to cut off an escape-route of the Gnostics, Ireneus continues:

"But if they say—as some of them do indeed say—that being inside and being outside of the Pleroma are to be understood in terms of knowing and of not-knowing respectively, since whoever knows something is

[12] Clem. Alex., *Strom.*, VIII, 2 ff; Stählin III, 81 ff.
[13] *Adv. Haer.*, II, 1, 5; Harvey I, 253 f.

within that which he knows, then they will have to admit that the Saviour himself (whom they call the All) was in a state of ignorance . . . If therefore, the Saviour went outside of the Pleroma, in order to search for the lost sheep, then he went outside of knowledge, and so he was in ignorance. For either they must admit that he was spatially outside of the Pleroma, and then we bring all our earlier arguments against them; or else, understanding inside and outside in terms of knowledge and ignorance respectively, they will have to admit that he whom they acknowledge as Saviour, and much earlier, Christ, were in ignorance, having gone outside of the Pleroma (that is, outside of knowledge), in order to form their mother".[14]

To reinforce the point, let us add the following passages from the *Excerpta ex Theodoto*, which recent editors ascribe not to Theodotus the Gnostic, but rather to Clement of Alexandria:[15]

". . . 'for I say to you that their (the children's) angels look always on the face of God' . . . 'Blessed are the pure of heart, for they shall see God'. But how can he, who has no shape, have a face? The apostle spoke of heavenly bodies, beautiful and intelligent; how could he have given them their different names, unless they had shape and form, unless, indeed, they were clothed in some body? 'The splendor of the heavenly bodies is different from that of terrestrial bodies, the splendor of the angels' bodies is different from both, and the splendor of the archangels' is different again': compared with the terrestral bodies, or with the stars, the angels and archangels are without shape, and incorporeal, but compared with the Son they can be said to be determinate bodies, accessible to sense. And the same can be said of the Son, compared with the Father. . .".[16]

". . . But it is through the Son, who is called the face of the Father, that the Father can be seen. The angels are intelligent fire, intelligent spirits who are perfectly purified; but the greatest thing that emerges from perfectly purified intelligent fire is intelligent light . . . The purity of the Son, however, is greater still, for he is light inaccessible, and the power of God . . . his clothes shone like light, but his face shone like the sun at which it is very difficult to look directly".[17]

[14] *Adv. Haer.*, II, 5, 2; Harvey I, 262.
[15] R. P. Casey, *The Excerpta ex Theodoto of Clement of Alexandria*, London, 1934, pp. 14 ff. F. Sagnard, *Clément d'Alexandrie, Extraits de Théodote*, Paris, 1948. SC 23, pp. 12 ff.
[16] *Excerpta ex Theodoto*, 11.
[17] *Ibid.*, 12.

"The demons are said to be incorporeal, not in the sense that they have no bodies at all (for they do have some form and shape, and therefore suffer the torments of sense); but in comparison with those bodies that are saved, the demons are said to be without bodies, since they, in comparison with the spiritual bodies, are as shadows. And the angels have bodies, for they are perceived by sight. Even the soul itself is a body; that is why the apostle says: What is sown is an animal body, but what is raised up is a spiritual body. And how can the souls that are being punished have any feeling, if they have no bodies? Fear him, therefore, says Christ, who after death can cast both body and soul into gehenna. But the body that appears to our senses is not purified by fire—it returns to earth. And on the other hand, the story of Lazarus and the rich man, with its references to parts of the body, shows clearly that the soul is a body".[18]

Clearly enough, these passages from the *Excerpta* not only give expression to a naive realism, grounded in a confusion to which men are naturally prone;[19] but they also appeal to the scriptures in support of this naive realism. And the same is to be said of Ireneus.[20] But there is a further element to be mentioned, and that is the influence of the Stoics. For on the basis of their own naive realism the Stoics had elaborated a whole system of materialistic philosophy; and many of the ante-Nicene authors, having quite an affinity with the Stoics, were moved to borrow

[18] *Ibid.*, 14. In the succeeding excerpt, the fifteenth, the same conclusion is drawn from 1 Cor. 15, 49 and 1 Cor. 13, 12. In an earlier excerpt, the tenth, certain general principles are laid down. The angels, the archangels and, it would appear, even the Son himself, are not without form, without aspect, without shape, without a body. They are not unsubstantial (ἀνούσιος), although the bodies that they have are not like the bodies on our earth. That which sees and is seen cannot be without shape, and incorporeal; however, the eye with which they see is not an eye of sense, it is the eye of intelligence, given by the Father.

[19] For just as men develop first as animals, before they reach the stage of rational deliberation and action, so they are more inclined to use sense and instinct, rather than intelligence and reason, in discriminating between what is real and what is imaginary.

[20] Cf. Iren., *Adv. Haer.*, II, 34, 1; Harvey I, 381, where the finger of Lazarus and the tongue of the rich man are used to prove that the separated souls, though separated, have bodily shapes.

their technical terms, and to adapt their distinctions and their theorems to their own ends.[21]

Now if error seeks supporting arguments in scripture and, at the same time, decks itself out in the terms and the distinctions of a philosophy, it can hardly be overcome except by a doctrine of hermeneutics, combined with an opposing philosophy. And this, in fact, is what happened at Alexandria. Clement himself, having discoursed at length, and with an abundance of illustrations, on the use of symbols,[22] boldly concluded:

> "Let no one, then, think that the Hebrews really attributed hands and feet and eyes and a mouth to God, or that they thought of him as really coming in and going out, or being angry and issuing threats. It is more pious to believe that some of these words are used allegorically".[23]
>
> "We must not even *think* of the Father of all as having a shape, or as moving, or as standing or sitting, or as being in some place, or as having a left and a right hand, *even though the scriptures say these things about him*".[24]

It is not enough, however, to recognise symbolic language as symbolic, unless one then goes on to say what the symbols mean. And if the symbols refer to God, who is incorporeal, this further step can hardly be taken without raising philosophic issues. And so, while for Ireneus and Hippolytus, and even for Epiphanius, the Greek philosophers were nothing but a source of errors,[25] Clement held a very different opinion:

[21] The extent of this Stoic "influence" is explained by M. Spanneut, *Le Stoicisme des Pères de l'Église*, De Clément de Rome à Clément d'Alexandrie, Paris, 1957.

[22] Clem. Alex., *Strom.*, V, 4–10; 19–66; MG 9, 37–101; Stählin II, 338–370.

[23] *Ibid.*, V, 11; 68, 3; MG 9, 103 B; Stählin II, 371, 18 ff.

[24] *Ibid.*, 71, 4; MG 110 A1; Stählin II, 374, 15.

[25] The judgment of Ireneus was that more than anything else the Gnostic systems were like those thought up by a certain comedian named Antiphanes. Still, he recognised in these systems some similarities to Thales, Homer, Anaximander, Anaxagoras, Democritus, Epicurus, Plato, Empedocles and the Pythagoreans; from this, however, he argued that if what the Greeks said was true, then the coming of Our Lord was pointless, and if what they said was false, then why should the Gnostics have believed them? [*Adv. Haer.*, II, 14, 1–6; Harvey I, 287–299; cf. the names of philosophers that appear in Harvey's

"So it appears that the liberal arts of the Greeks, along with philosophy itself, came to man from God. Not that God is the immediate source of the liberal arts and of philosophy, so that all of their products should be attributed directly to him—think rather of the rain, which pours down not only on good earth, but also on dung, and on people's dwellings. . . . By philosophy I mean not the Stoic or Platonic or Epicurean or Aristotelian school, but a selection from them of what was correctly said and taught justice along with pious knowledge (τοῦτο σύμπαν τὸ ἐκλεκτικόν). The other elements, which are the adulterated fruit of human reasoning, these I would never call divine".[26]

However, Clement did more than draw a distinction, in the Greek sources, between what the Greeks had received from God and what was the corrupt fruit of natural human powers; he himself thought out and formulated a new kind of inquiry:

"Even the ancient philosophers were not moved by a spirit of contentiousness, doubting everything they heard; much less should we be, who embrace the true philosophy, who are also clearly commanded by scripture to investigate things thoroughly, in order to discover more. The more recent Greek philosophers, impelled by a longing for empty praise, spend their time in arguments and refutations of arguments, and end up in trivialities. Our barbarian philosophy, on the other hand, has no place for any sort of strife. What it says is: 'Seek, and you shall find; knock, and it shall be opened to you; ask, and you shall receive' (Mt 7,7; Lk 11,9) Investigation by question and answer is, I think, knocking on the door of truth, asking that it be opened. When the door, which had been barring the way, is opened by investigation, scientific contemplation of the truth begins (ἐπιστημονική θεωρία). I believe that to those who knock on the door in this manner, what they seek to understand is opened up. And to those who ask, in this way, following the command of scripture, God grants what they

---

index.] The aim of Hippolytus, in composing his *Refutation of All Heresies*, was that having first expounded the opinions of the astrologers and the philosophers, he might the more easily demonstrate that the heretics, far from teaching divine knowledge, taught nothing new at all—what they taught was nothing but errors, and ancient errors at that [MG 16[3], 3018 ff; Wendland, I ff, 52 ff; but see Altaner, 184 f]. Epiphanius, finally, went so far as to list the Stoics, the Platonists, the Pythagoreans and the Epicureans among the heretics [*Haer.*, V-VIII: MG 41, 201 ff; Holl I, 183 ff].

[26] Clem. Alex., *Strom.*, I, 7; 37, i.6; MG 8, 731 B and D; Stählin II, 24.

seek: their inquiry truly sheds light on what they are investigating, and from God they receive a full understanding of it. For it is impossible that one should find, without having sought, or should seek without investigating, or, asking questions, should fail to open up, explain, and make clear the thing that he seeks to understand. Again, it is impossible that he who proceeds by careful investigation should fail to receive his reward, namely, the particular knowledge that he seeks. But the one who will find is the one who has sought; and the one who seeks is the one who considers that he does not know. Such a person, impelled by a longing to discover what is beautiful, seeks calmly, not in any spirit of contentiousness, and without desire for personal glory, proceeding by question and answer, and considering carefully what is said. And it is not only those who apply themselves to the study of sacred scripture who have to raise and order questions in a proper manner, so that their inquiry may lead to some profitable conclusion; for the same applies to those who are concerned with ordinary matters. Turbulent men with clever rhetoric have their own place and their own audience, but not here. He who is both a lover and a disciple of the truth must be a man of peace: in all of his investigations he must proceed by scientific demonstration, without excessive self-love, but loving only the truth, and so advance towards comprehensive understanding (γνῶσις καταληπτική)".[27]

In his own manner, Clement here anticipates the doctrine proclaimed by the first Vatican council: "Reason illumined by faith, when it inquires diligently, piously, soberly, reaches with God's help some extremely fruitful understanding of the mysteries . . ." (DS 3016). For he urges a methodical ordering of questions and answers, which is certainly proper to reason. But what inspires him is his belief that Jesus, who said "Seek, and you shall find", will enlighten well-ordered inquiry and bestow its reward, and this is something like the notion of reason illumined by faith. At least it recalls the request of Solomon for Wisdom (1 Kings 3, 5–15).

6. The development of the concept of God.

The movement away from a literal to an allegorical interpretation of scripture and the introduction of a kind of philo-

[27] Strom., VIII, 1; MG 9, 558 ff; Stählin III, 80 f.

sophic mode of inquiry could hardly fail to have some effect on the manner of conceiving God. To this topic we now turn, which brings us closer to the topic of trinitarian doctrine.

In the early Christian centuries belief in one, supreme God was quite common among the educated classes. The Stoics, however, held that this one God was the soul of the world, an intelligent fire that burned without consuming, a part of the material universe, although its active and its principal part. The Platonists, on the other hand, identified God with the supreme, subsistent Idea of the Good; some of them identified this supreme Idea with the Demiurge, who made everything else, but others said that Plato, in the *Timaeus*, introduced the Demiurge only as a kind of mythical character.[28] The Gnostics, for their part, were so insistent on the transcendence and unknowability of God that for them the Demiurge was an inferior being, outside of the Pleroma, belonging not to the class of the "pneumatics", who are saved necessarily, but to that of the "psychics", whose fate is uncertain. For the Marcionites, finally, the Demiurge was that severe God of the Old Testament, from whom the good God of the New Testament purchased us.

Against all such conceptions of God Ireneus writes:

"... there is only this one God, who made all things, who alone is omnipotent, who alone is Father, making and establishing all things, visible and invisible 'in the word of his power', This is the one, only God, maker of the world, who is above every principality, and above all other supernatural powers. He is the Father, he is God, he is the creator who made all things through himself, that is, through his own Word and his own Wisdom—heaven and earth, and the seas, and all that is in them. He it is who is just and good; he it is who formed man and planted paradise, who made the world, who sent the flood, and saved Noah; he is the God of Abraham, the God of Isaac, and the God of Jacob, the God of the living, whom the Law proclaims, whose praises the Prophets sing, whom Christ

[28] On the cultural situation among the pagans, A. J. Festugière, *La Révélation d'Hermès Trismégiste*, 4 vol., Paris, 1949–1954; especially vol. 2, on the cosmic God and vol. 4, on the unknown God. On the Platonists, especially the so-called Middle Platonists, Hal Koch, *Pronoia und Paideusis*, Berlin, 1932. On the Stoics, M. Spanneut, *Le Stoïcisme des Pères*, 1957.

THE WAY TO NICEA

reveals, about whom the Apostles teach, and in whom the Church believes. He is the Father of our Lord, Jesus Christ; through his Word, which is his Son, he is revealed and made manifest to those to whom he is revealed: for they know him, to whom the Son has revealed him. . . .".[29]

In the conception of God presented here by Ireneus there are three elements to be distinguished. In the first place, there was the traditional Hebrew notion that God became known as a person identified with certain historical events: he was the God of the Patriarchs, the God of the Law and the God of the Prophets. Secondly, there was the extension and amplification of this notion, contained in the New Testament: the same God is also the Father of our Lord, Jesus Christ, the God of the gospel, the God of the apostolic preaching, the God of the Church, and the God of each individual Christian's religious experience. Thirdly, there was the doctrine, common to the Old and the New Testaments, that this God is supreme, that he is the Lord, the maker and shaper and sustainer of absolutely all things, and of all persons without exception, to whom no one else can even be compared, much less be considered his equal.

Now all three of these elements can equally be conceived as objects of faith; the third, however, is not beyond the grasp of natural human reason, and this is a point that did not escape either Justin or Ireneus, both of whom had some inkling of the distinction between faith itself and the preambles of faith. For as Ireneus wrote:

"Justin says well, in his book against Marcion: 'For I would not have believed the Lord himself if he had announced some other God than him who created and sustains us. But because there came to us, from the one God who made this world and fashioned us, who holds and controls all things, because from this one God there came his only-begotten Son, drawing all things together in himself, therefore my faith in him is firm, and my love of the Father unshakeable, God himself bestowing both on us'".[30]

One must not, of course, transpose this into a much later theological context, to infer that these ancient Christian writers

[29] Iren., *Adv. Haer.*, II, 30, 0; Harvey I, 368.
[30] Iren., *Adv. Haer.*, IV, 6, 2; Harvey II, 158 f.

had drawn a sharp distinction between reason and faith, and between fundamental and dogmatic theology. On the other hand, neither can what they said be reduced to a mere fideism.

What exactly was the content of this preliminary notion of God, that was somehow to be presupposed in every discussion, and in every later development? There are many indications that the basic notion was of God as omnipotent; this omnipotence, however, was considered rather in its actual exercise than in the range of its possible application, and (more or less in the biblical manner) with little or no distinction made between substance, active potency, and activity itself.[31] For in the scriptures the Father is most commonly called the Lord [κύριος], as is the Son, and the earliest Christians retained this usage. Next, according to Eusebius[32] Justin composed a work (not extant) entitled *On the Monarchy*.[33] Theophilus of Antioch also, and more than once, spoke of the monarchy of God. And the doctrine of the Patripassians, that the Father and the Son are the same person, is said to have been based not on the affirmation of the unity of the divine essence, but rather on their determination to safeguard the monarchy.[34] Tertullian, however, saw a grave danger that the mass of simple Christians would be deceived by such an argument;[35] he himself considered that it was a sufficient refut-

[31] For a comparison between Greek and Hebrew mentalities, see the evidence adduced and the comments made by A. Grillmeier, *Scholastik*, 33 (1958), 554 ff, indeed from p. 547.

[32] Euseb., HE IV, 18, 3; not to be confused with the spurious work that editors sometimes attribute to Justin.

[33] Monarchy means power possessed by one person; omnipotence means power that extends over everybody. Evans, *Treatise against Praxeas*, p. 6, gathered a lot of material on the notion of monarchy, and he held that it was opposed to polytheism. Likewise Prestige, *God in Patristic Thought*, pp. 94 ff. See J. Daniélou (*Gospel message . . .*, pp. 346–353) on the term, δύναμις, as used by Justin and other apologists.

[34] Tert., *Adv. Prax.*, 3; Evans, 91, 19: " 'We uphold the monarchy', they say".

[35] *Ibid.*, 3; 91, 9: "The simple people, not to say the unwise and unlearned, who always constitute the majority of believers, become terrified at the thought of the economy [of Three in one]."

ation of the Patripassians to say that monarchy consisted not in the oneness of a ruler, but in the oneness of rule.[36] Dionysius of Rome, finally, called the doctrine of the monarchy the most august doctrine of the Church.[37] And one might add that Ireneus, writing against the Gnostics about the one God, who is the creator of all, seems to come to his most fundamental point when he concludes that the opinion of his adversaries leads to "the voiding of the name, Omnipotent, and such an opinion necessarily ends up in impiety".[38] Further, we have already seen the argument of Hippolytus, that the trinity does not destroy the divine unity, because the power of the three Persons is one. And Clement of Alexandria considered that other names of God (for example, One, Good, Mind, That-itself-which-is, Father, God, Creator, Lord) taken not singly, but all together, indicate the power of the Omnipotent.[39] Finally, as we remarked before, the contribution of Origen to this whole discussion lies in the area of exegesis, rather than of metaphysics.[40]

Clement of Alexandria also set about explaining more precisely how one should conceive God:

"... if we abstract from all the natural qualities of a body, first from its depth, then from its breadth, and then from its length, we are left with a concept of what we might call unity with position. By abstracting, further, from position, we reach the notion of unity itself. If then, abstracting from all the qualities of bodies, and of the things we call incorporeal, we cast ourselves into the magnitude of Christ, and, thence, in holiness, advance into his immensity, we reach some slight understanding of the Omnipotent; not that we understand what it is, but rather what it is not".[41]

In order, then, to reach some understanding of the Omnipotent, one first abstracts all that is sensible and corporeal; then one takes

[36] *Ibid.*, 3; 91, 22 ff.
[37] DS 112. Cf. the Apostles' Creed, DS 10 ff.
[38] Iren., *Adv. Haer.*, II, 1, 5; Harvey I, 254.
[39] Hippolytus is cited above, pp. 50 ff. Clement below, p. 123.
[40] See above, pp. 56 ff. cf. pp. 63 f.
[41] Clem. Alex., *Strom.*, V, 11; 71, 2, 3; MG 9, 107 B; Stählin II, 374.

a kind of pious leap; but what one comes to know is not what God is, but rather what he is not. Clement inculcated this rather negative theology both in his general assertion that God is "above place and time and name and understanding",[42] and also, spelling it out in greater detail, in the following passage:

"Neither can one rightly say that he is the whole; for 'the whole' is used to describe what has magnitude, and it does not fit him who is the Father of the whole universe . . . And one cannot say that he has any parts. He is infinite, not in the sense that he is some vast expanse which can never be traversed, but because he has no dimensions, and therefore no limits. Therefore, he is without shape, and he cannot be named. If at times we do—in an applied sense—name him, calling him one, or good, or mind, or that-itself-which-is, or Father, or God, or Creator, or Lord, we do so not as giving out his proper name; rather because we do not know his proper name, we use these other beautiful names in order to focus our thought on them, and prevent it from going astray. For although these names, taken singly, do not signify God, taken all together they suggest the power of the Omnipotent. For names denote either the accidental qualities or the relationships of things, and nothing of this sort can be said of God; for such knowledge proceeds from what is prior and better known, but there is nothing before the unbegotten. It remains, therefore, certainly, that it is by the grace of God, and only through his Word, that we come to understand the unknown God himself. This is the meaning of Paul's 'To the unknown God', recalled by Luke in the Acts of the Apostles".[43]

Clement's position, then, is this: first, in order to come to knowledge of the Omnipotent we must abstract from everything corporeal; second, we can have no proper knowledge of him, either by understanding the names we give him or by demonstration *a priori*; and third, we can indeed reach some understanding of him, through the grace of God himself and through the Word.

Origen, following in Clement's footsteps, and as if suspecting that there could still be some lingering doubt about the matter in some people's minds, undertook a systematic refutation of

[42] *Ibid.*, 71, 5; MG 110 A; Stählin II, 374.
[43] *Ibid.*, V, 12; 81, 5–82, 4; MG 9, 122 f; Stählin II, 380 f.

the notion that God was a body.[44] He called the Son wisdom itself, in order to make it understood that he was neither something unsubstantial nor, on the other hand, a body;[45] and although in general he doubted that any rational creature could live entirely without a body—at least some finer, less crass kind of body—he totally excluded the Blessed Trinity from this general rule. The following passage is rather long, but it is worth transcribing here, so well does it reveal both the mind and the method of Origen:

"At this point some ask whether, as the Father generates the Son and brings forth the Spirit, but not in the sense that they did not previously exist—since in the Trinity there is no before and after—but in the sense that the Father is the origin and source of the Son and the Spirit, whether there might not be a similar sort of communion or closeness between rational creatures and corporeal matter. To investigate the matter more fully and carefully, they begin by asking whether this corporeal nature itself, which supports the life and contains the motions of spiritual and rational minds, will also share in their eternity, or whether, separated from them, it will perish and go to earth. To get a more precise grasp of the matter, it seems that we must first ask, whether it is at all possible for rational natures, when they have come to the peak of holiness and blessedness, to remain without bodies—which to me seems very difficult, if not impossible, to maintain—or whether they must always remain joined to bodies. If someone were to explain how they could in fact be entirely without bodies, then it would follow that corporeal nature was created from nothing, for periods of time, so that, just as from not-being it came into being, in the same way, when its service was no longer required, it ceased to be.

"However, if it cannot at all be affirmed that any nature, excepting the Father, the Son, and the Holy Spirit, can live apart from the body, then, led by reason, we are forced to the conclusion that while it is, first and foremost, rational creatures that were created, still it is only in thought that material substance can be separated from them; to our way of thinking, it was made for them and after them, but they never did and never do live without it, for only the life of the Trinity can be rightly thought to be in-

[44] Orig., *De princ.*, I, 1; Koetschau, 16–27.
[45] *Ibid.*, I, 2, 2; Koetschau, 28, 13 ff.

corporeal. Therefore, as we have said above, that material substance, being by nature such that it is transformed from one thing into another, when it is drawn to beings of a lower order, becomes a more crass and solid kind of body and serves to distinguish the visible species of this world in all their variety; but when it is at the service of more perfect and more blessed beings, it shines in the splendor of the 'heavenly bodies', and, in the vesture of 'the spiritual body', it adorns 'the angels of God' or 'the children of the resurrection', all of whom together will fill out the variety and the diversity of the one world.

"But if we are to discuss this topic more fully, we must, with greater care and diligence, and with all due fear of God, and with all due reverence, examine the sacred scriptures: first assembling all the relevant passages, and then seeing if perhaps we can find in them some secret and hidden meaning concerning these things, something hidden away, which 'the Holy Spirit makes clear' to those who are worthy".[46]

It is clear from this passage that Origen was not enough of a speculative thinker to conceive that there could be anything incorporeal in God's creation. It is also clear that he was so much an exegete that he considered that a fuller understanding of the matter was to be sought, with all due fear of God and with all due reverence, in the scriptures themselves. Let us look, at least, at a single sample of the method he used, and the great care he took, in examining the scriptures himself. Commenting on the first verse of the prologue to St. John's Gospel, he asserted that it is not enough to ask in what sense Christ is the Word, while leaving out of account all of his other titles, such as, the light of the world, the way, the truth and the life, the good shepherd, I am he, who speaks with you, the master, the Lord, the Son of God, the door, the true vine, the bread of life, the living bread, the first and the last, Alpha and Omega, the beginning and the end, the light of the gentiles, the servant of Jahwe, and, as he said, thousands more.[47] Origen himself looked for a synthesis of all of these; he recognised that there was a distinction of reason between them;[48] he affirmed that "Wisdom" was older than all

---

[46] Orig., *De princ.*, II, 2; Koetschau, 111, 28–113, 10.

[47] Orig., *In Joan.*, I, 21 (23); Preuschen, 25, 21 ff.

[48] *Ibid.*, I, 9 (11); Preuschen, 14, 12–22.

of the other titles;[49] and he went, more or less systematically, through the whole list of titles.[50]

However, no one who reflects at all can assemble and order titles in this way, without at least giving some hint as to what that reality is, to which the titles are to be attributed. Origen's solution to this fundamental problem was predominantly Platonist: the Father was divinity itself and goodness itself; the Son, on the other hand, was the Word itself, wisdom itself, truth itself, the resurrection-and-the-life itself, but the Father was something better than all of these, something unknown to us.[51] If one asks how these Platonic ideas could then be brought together and united with each other, while being associated with the two distinct hypostases of the Father and the Son, the answer would seem to lie in the eclecticism of that time:[52] as well as taking over the categories of the Platonists, Origen also borrowed from Stoic materialism the notions of *ousia* and *hypostasis*.[53] If one urges that this is hardly consistent, then one has come to the basic difficulty, which can be explained in two ways. For, in the first place, as we remarked above, Hal Koch believes that one cannot insist too strongly that Origen was not a metaphysician, in the proper sense of the term. Secondly, however, the point must be made differently, more from a theological point of view. For, while Origen accepted with his whole heart both the truth of the scriptures and the preaching of the Church,[54] what he sought above all was a spiritual meaning, going beyond

[49] *Ibid.*, I, 19 (22); Preuschen, 24, 20 ff.

[50] *Ibid.*, 21–38; Preuschen, 25–50.

[51] See above, pp. 61 ff.

[52] Hal Koch, *op. cit.*, p. 268: "Our investigation has shown that Albinus and Origen represent essentially the same form of eclectic Platonism, sharing a kind of basic Platonic horizon, with numerous Aristotelian and Stoic elements added in. They manifest a wide-ranging similarity in terminology, and they are taken up to a large extent with the same problems, to which they provide essentially the same solutions. In brief: they belong to the same school".

[53] A. Orbe, *Primera teología*, pp. 431–448, especially the schemata and note 55, p. 447.

[54] Above, pp. 56 ff.

the totality of literal meaning.[55] Unfortunately, however, neither in the philosophers nor by his own efforts did he find any sure criterion by which to judge the truth of this spiritual meaning. This failure of his should cause us no surprise, since the doctrine expounded in Plato's dialogues is aimed essentially at raising the mind above the things of sense, generating enthusiasm for spiritual things and replacing myth with better myths; but it contains so little understanding of the Yes, Yes, and No, No of the gospel, that both being and non-being are also reduced to ideas.[56]

7. The Development of Trinitarian Doctrine

If we examine the doctrine of the Blessed Trinity in the developed form represented by the determinations of the council of Nicea we can distinguish in it three main elements. In the first place there was the revealed name, Son; many other titles were applied to Christ but from the beginning he was called "Son" in a very special sense. The second element, derived from both the Old and the New Testaments, is the insistence, against the Gnostics and the Marcionites, that there is no distinction between God the Creator and the true God, and the insistence that the one, true God is radically distinct from all creatures.[57] From both of these elements taken together it follows that the Son, who was also acknowledged as maker and Lord and judge of all, is truly Son, born of the Father, and cannot be considered a part of creation.[58]

However, the decree of Nicea would appear to contain a third element quite distinct from the first two, namely, the ontological mentality that finds expression in the affirmation that the Son is

---

[55] For a brief discussion, P. Nemeshegyi, "Le Dieu d'Origène et le Dieu de l'Ancient Testament", N.R. Th., 80 (1958), 495–509.

[56] Plato, Sophistes, 258 c. Cf. Insight, p. 365 f.

[57] Cf. the Apostles' Creed, DS 10 ff, where there is a declaration of faith in one God, the Father almighty, παντοκράτορα, creator of heaven and earth. On the origin of this creed, see Altaner, pp. 47–50.

[58] Cf. Dionysius of Rome, DS 113 f.

consubstantial with the Father. For to speak of God as creator, to speak of him as "Lord of all' is to speak in terms of his relative attributes, using categories that resonate with religious experience: when we speak of God in this way we also affirm our total dependence on him. On the other hand, to speak of the Son as consubstantial with the Father is to consider the divinity in itself, going beyond religious experience to employ or to suppose the scientific categories of an ontology. And since this mode of speech has long been a major stumbling block, giving many people the impression that the Church at Nicea had abandoned the genuine Christian doctrine, which was religious through and through, in order to embrace some sort of hellenistic ontology, we must examine the matter with some care.[59]

In the first place, there is nothing in the Old or in the New Testament that is clearer than this, that the word of God, the word announced by the prophets when they said, "Thus says the Lord . . ." is to be preserved intact by the Apostles in accordance with the precept, "Let your word be 'Yes, Yes' and 'No, No'" (Mt 5, 37), and that this same word not only was preached by the apostles but was also to be preserved in all its purity, even to the extent that any other word, even if preached by an angel, was to be anathema (Gal 1, 8).

Now this word of God not only grounds the dogmatism of the Church, which cuts off heretics with the celebrated formula, "If anyone says . . . let him be anathema"; it also contains implicitly a certain dogmatic realism. In order to explain what this means we shall have to consider in turn the words "realism", "dogmatic" and "implicitly".

In the first place, then, the word of God contains a realism, both because it is to be believed and not contradicted, and also because it is a true word, telling of things as in fact they are. For realism consists in this, that the truth that is acknowledged in the mind corresponds to reality. But whoever believes the true word of God certainly acknowledges truth in his mind—indeed his

---

[59] On the history of this question, see A. Grillmeier, "Hellenisierung-Judaisierung . . .", *Scholastik*, 33 (1958), 321–355; 528–558.

adherence to this truth is so complete that he banishes from his thoughts even the slightest suspicion that things might be other than as God has revealed them to be.

Secondly, this kind of realism is dogmatic, not only in the sense that it belongs to the very essence of dogma, but also in the sense that it is not the product of any philosophic reflection. To the extent that one is a philosopher one will make no affirmation for which one cannot assign sufficient and cogent reasons. But the realism that is found in the word of God as revealed, preached and accepted does not consist in any further philosophic reflection; it is simply a matter of sincere acceptance of the word of God that has been revealed and preached.

Thirdly, while this dogmatic realism is contained in the word of God, it is present only implicitly, not acknowledged explicitly. We are not saying that Isaiah, Paul and Athanasius knew that they were dogmatic realists. We are not saying that they made clear distinctions between the good and the true, and the will and the mind, and so between the mind itself and the reality to which the mind's truth corresponds. Much less are we saying that they drew all the consequences that would follow from these distinctions. What in fact we are saying is that these men had minds, that they knew the word of God and that they lived according to the reality that they came to know through God's true word.

After these preliminary remarks we may return to the question whether the Church, in the decree of the council of Nicea, went beyond the categories of religious experience to embrace a hellenistic ontology. The question, of course, has its own presuppositions: leaving out of account the word of God, it makes a disjunction between religious experience on the one hand and hellenistic ontology on the other. However, if such presuppositions are appropriate to rationalists and liberal theologians, for whom the word of God is but an archaic, not to say mythical, mode of speech, they cannot be admitted by those who accept the word of God in faith; neither can they be admitted by those historians who conceive history not as a disguised polemic but as a science that seeks to understand the mentality of another age. For what Isaiah felt compelled to announce, and Paul to preach, and Athanasius to defend, was not just a personal religious experience, but the word of God, and the categories of religious experience are not the same as those contained implicitly in the word of God. For there is no doubt that the categories derived from religious experience will contain a reference to the subject who has the experience, but "the word of God is not tied", restricted to speaking of things as related to us and unable to speak of things as they are in themselves. For one cannot exclude, *a priori*, from the range of God's word anything that can be affirmed or denied through human words, on the ground that a particular kind of affirmation or denial does not fit into the categories of what we call religious experience.

Moreover, the Nicene concept of consubstantiality does not go beyond the dogmatic realism that is contained implicitly in the word of God. For it means no more than this, that what is said of the Father is to be said also of the Son, except that the Son is Son and not Father. But what is said of the Father is certainly said: there are propositions that are to be believed and that, being true, correspond to reality. Equally, what is said of the Son are certain propositions that are to be believed and that correspond to reality. And if, excluding from the former set the propositions that apply to the Father, one affirms that the remainder coincide with those that apply to the Son, this further affirmation also remains entirely within the field of dogmatic realism. But in making this further affirmation one has affirmed that the Son is consubstantial with the Father.

There is no need, then, to speak of the importation of a hellenistic ontology.[60] Indeed, the more carefully one examines the

[60] Besides, it must be remarked that as well as many philosophers and theologians, there are also many very learned historians who make no real distinction between metaphysics and myth, since for them metaphysics is simply scientifically elaborated myth (e.g. P. Tillich RGG² IV, 437). So if one finds some author deriving the teaching of the council of Nicea from Gnosticism, one can often discover the fallacy more quickly by examining his philosophical presuppositions, rather than going directly to the historical documents.

brands of hellenistic ontology that were actually available at the time, the more obviously superfluous does any such hypothesis appear. In Tertullian one can detect a hellenistic ontology of Stoic inspiration, but the measure of its presence is precisely the measure of Tertullian's removal from the Nicene notion of consubstantiality. In Origen too one can find a hellenistic ontology, derived rather from Platonism, but its tendency is to place Origen at an even greater remove than Tertullian from the doctrine of Nicea. And Arius, no less than Athanasius, rejected both the Valentinian notion of emission and the Manichean notion of consubstantial part.

We do not mean to suggest that the dogmatic realism, contained implicitly in the word of God, became an explicit realism, without any contributory influence of hellenistic culture. It is one thing to seek the source of dogmatic realism and quite another to assign the causes whereby an implicit philosophic position became to some extent explicit. If there had been no Gnostics, no Marcionites, no Sabellians and no Arians and, on the other hand, no bishops who thought that heretics were to be answered not only by excommunication but also by a precisely formulated profession of Faith, then the formula for the consubstantiality of the Son would scarcely have been discovered. And one cannot explain the Gnostics, the Marcionites, the Sabellians, the Arians, or the bishops who reasoned as they did, without acknowledging the influence on all of them of hellenistic culture. This influence, however, has been recognised and affirmed since the Patristic age; far from supplying proof that the Church substituted for the Christian religion some other kind of religion, it merely assigns the cause, prepared by divine providence, whereby the Christian religion itself was enabled to make explicit what from the beginning was contained implicitly in the word of God itself.

To make this process of increasing explicitness a little clearer we must compare three different kinds of realism: naive realism, dogmatic realism and critical realism. All men claim to know the real, but when it comes to assigning the grounds for this common conviction it appears very clearly that different people have different criteria of reality. For example, naive realists say they know that this very obvious mountain is real because with their eyes they can see it, with their feet they can tread on it, with their hands they can handle it, and since to them the matter is so patently clear, they will attribute either to silliness or to perversity every effort to find, or urge to offer, any further ground for their conviction. Critical realists, on the other hand, while conceding that this same mountain is indeed visible to the eye, firm under foot and palpable to the hand, nonetheless add that as visible, firm and palpable it is only sensed—that it is not known as real until by a true judgment it is affirmed to exist. Since this—at least to naive realists—is anything but obvious, critical realists go on to investigate the matter thoroughly, piling up convincing reasons for each of their assertions and cutting off all avenues of escape from their position. Dogmatic realists, finally, whether in virtue of a strong natural endowment of reasonableness (this would appear, however, to be the exception) or else being schooled implicitly by the revealed word of God, agree with the critical realists, but without being able to explain just why they do, whence it can quite easily come about that, mixing naive realism in with their dogmatic realism, they land themselves in inconsistency.

This kind of mixture of dogmatic and naive realism is easily detectable in the ante-Nicene Christian authors. For they who were so committed to the word of God that they spread the Christian Faith throughout the Roman empire, at the cost, for so many of them, of dying martyrs' deaths, were assuredly, if implicitly, dogmatic realists: far from taking as the sole reality the world revealed to the senses, they clung above all else to that reality made known to them by God's true word. The dogmatic realist, however, is unable, as we have have said, to explain his own position adequately; likewise, he has little or no grasp of the implications of that position. He is sure that the real is known through true judgment but at the same time he adds that by its bulk it occupies a determinate part of space. He has no doubt that those things are distinct of which one is not the other, but he also adds that those things are distinct that are in different places and as well, perhaps, at different times. It is quite clear to him that effects depend on causes, but he also has a need to see the dependence of effect on cause: branches growing out of a tree, or offspring born of parent, or brightness emitted by the sun, or a torch lit from another torch.

This internally inconsistent mixture of dogmatic and naive realism provides what we called above[61] the material foundation for the process of dialectic.

The formal principle of that same dialectic cannot fail to be at hand—it consists in the light of natural reason, either illumined or unillumined by Faith. Therefore, given the appropriate occasions, which heretics are apt to provide, the objective dialectic process itself is calculated to drive out naive realism and in so doing to bring dogmatic realism to a greater self-consciousness.

However, since the dogmatic realism that we speak of was only implicit, the dialectic process also was only implicit; it was not grounded philosophically, but worked itself out in the handling of religious and theological questions. Or, to express the matter differently: from the beginning the word of God contained within it an implicit epistemology and ontology, but what was there implicitly became known explicitly only through dialectic process that was spread over time; and this dialectic process was all the more complex, as the real roots of the problem were touched only indirectly.

There was a first movement, begun in the New Testament itself, that was an exploration of the mutual relationships of the Law and the Gospel, according to the familiar principle that the New Testament lies concealed in the Old and the Old is made plain in the New; and to this were added the various apologies, some addressed to the Jews and some to the Gentiles. But among the new converts to Christianity there were, on the one hand, Jews who were as yet unable to transcend the Old Testament

[61] P. 48.

133

categories and kept insisting that Jesus was no more than a teacher, a prophet, or an angel. At the opposite pole there were the Gentile converts, to whom the Old Testament seemed sheer nonsense and who, therefore, basing themselves on the symbolic speculations of the Gnostics or the biblical criticism of the Marcionites, made a distinction between the much inferior Creator God and the supreme, good God. Thus arose two related problems about the manner of conceiving God, one a problem of hermeneutics and the other a problem of theology. Soon there was added a trinitarian problem; for when the Creator God of the Old Testament and God the Father of the New Testament and the supreme God, known by natural reason, had all three been identified with each other, along came those who were variously called Patripassians, Monarchians, Sabellians, to say that God the Father was the same person as God the Son.

To the challenge thus posed the Western Church responded in one way and the Alexandrians in quite another. The Western Fathers, hardly broaching at all the hermeneutical problem, insisted on the distinction between God the Creator and his Son; in the process of defending this distinction they manifested objectively their naive realism and they discovered the trinitarian formula, "of one substance". The Alexandrians, on the other hand, attacked the hermeneutical problem methodically and scientifically, they sought a way of getting beyond the scriptural symbols to the reality that they symbolised, and they overcame naive realism by adopting a form of Platonism, and so Origen would say that the Father was truly God, while the Son was God by participation.

Now if it is clear enough that the theology that arose in Alexandria and was brought by Origen to Caesarea was less than perfect, it is no less clear that the theology of Tertullian, Hippolytus, Novatian and Dionysius of Alexandria was not entirely without defect. What was needed was a kind of breakthrough, and this was finally brought about through the protracted Arian controversies.

Arius did three main things: 1) by ruling out all anthropomorphic or metaphorical language he took the ground from under naive realism; 2) setting aside the Platonic categories introduced by Origen, he posed the question at issue in the Christian categories of Creator and creature; 3) having thus set up the problem, he resolved it by arguing, in a more or less rationalistic manner, to the conclusion that the Son was a creature.

The Council of Nicea employed dogmatic realism. While it did not explicitly repudiate naive realism, it did so implicitly.[62] The council Fathers considered those phrases that might suggest Platonic participation, as for example that the Son is without difference most similar to the Father, but when they saw how the Arians could get around all such phrases, they rejected them.[63] Then, in direct opposition to the Arians, they laid down that the Son is not a creature, that he is not temporal, and that he is not mutable. Finally, in order to issue a positive statement of Catholic doctrine, they declared that the Son is both born of the Father and consubstantial with him.

The subsequent controversies show how inevitable all of this was. Within the council itself there were those who held that it was impossible for anything that was not a material, corporeal thing to be consubstantial with anything else; by parity of reasoning they would have said that it is impossible for anything that is not a material, corporeal thing to be a son; and the very use of the category of impossibility reveals a rationalistic turn of mind, with too little appreciation of the fact that there are mysteries in God.

Equally rationalistic were the Eusebians and Homoeousians, who could understand the Son's consubstantiality with the Father only in a Sabellian sense; more seriously so were the

[62] This can be seen clearly enough from the explanations given in the council itself, according to the account of Eusebius, *Epist. ad suae paroeciae homines* (AW III, 45 ff; MG 20, 1540 C ff), and from Athanasius, *De decretis nic. syn.* (AW II, 1–45; MG 25, 416–476), *passim.*

[63] Athan., *De decretis nic. syn.*, 20; AW II, 16, 27 ff; MG 25, 450 C. Cf. Alex. of Alexandria, *Epist. ad Alex. ep. Thess.*, AW III, 27, 15.

Anomoeans who, by fallacious syllogisms, attempted to demonstrate the impossibility of the Blessed Trinity.

The Long-lined Creed represents a theology that was at the time already antiquated; it contains an attempt to revive naive realism, establishing the unity of God by an appeal to monarchy, concord and the subordination of the Son, a natural conjunction and union of the Son with the Father, and a dependence on the Father.[64]

An equally antiquated theology appears in the Eusebians, who appealed to a type of Platonic participation, with little awareness of the fact that this participation of theirs was hellenistic, whereas the categories of Creator and creature were not hellenistic but Christian.

The Homoeans, finally, affirmed that the Son is similiar to the Father and they ruled out every use of ontological terms. However, they could not exclude from men's minds the question —still asked today as it was asked then—whether Christ, the Son of God, is himself also God, or a creature like us. But if, while not excluding the question, one excludes the possibility of an answer to the question, one is guilty of an archaism that supposes that people living in the present live not in the present but in some long-past age. Such an archaism is as harmful as it is mistaken, for indeed the times do change and we change with them.

Now if, when it emerged, the Nicene dogma was inevitable, it was nonetheless new. For it marks a transition from multiplicity to unity: from a multiplicity of symbols, titles and predicates to the ultimate ground of all of these, namely, the Son's consubstantiality with the Father. Equally, it marks a transition from things as related to us to things as they are in themselves, from the relational concepts of God as supreme agent, Creator, Omnipotent Lord of all, to an ontological conception of the divine substance itself. It marks, no less, a transition from the word of God as accommodated to particular people, at particular

---

[64] The *Long-lined Creed*, IX; Hahn, pp. 192 ff; Athan., *De syn.*, 26; AW II, 253, 34 ff; MG 26, 733 B.

times, under particular circumstances, to the word of God as it is to be proclaimed to all people, of all times, under whatever circumstances—the transition from the prophetic oracle of Yahweh, the gospel as announced in Galilee, the apostolic preaching and the simple tradition of the Church, from all of these to Catholic dogma. It also marks a transition from the mystery of God as hidden in symbols, hinted at by a multiplicity of titles, apprehended only in a vague and confused manner in the dramatico-practical pattern of experience, to the mystery of God as circumscribed and manifested in clear, distinct and apparently contradictory affirmations. Finally it marks a transition from a whole range of problems to a basic solution of those problems. For a definitive step was taken from naive realism, beyond Platonism, to dogmatic realism and in the direction of critical realism. To the hermeneutical question, what it is that symbols symbolise, it was answered that what they symbolise is that which is, that which is truly affirmed. To the theological question, how God was to be conceived, an answer was given that set aside the sublime Platonic Ideas, reaffirmed the omnipotent Creator and went beyond the notion of God as agent to think of him in terms of the substance that causes all substances, the being that is for all beings the source of their being. To the trinitarian question, finally, an answer was given that laid the foundation on which, of its own accord, as it were, the whole systematisation of Catholic theology would arise. Given that later systematisation, however, it is only with the greatest difficulty that we who have inherited it can come to understand how the ante-Nicene authors could in fact have said what in fact they did say.

INDEX OF NAMES

Duméry, H., 64
Duplacy, J., 18

Ebionites 18, 37, 94, 111
Eliade, M, 6
Elkesites, 18 f, 111
Empedocles, 116
Epicurus, 116 f
Epiphanius, 37, 39, 76, 78, 85, 94, 111
Euclid, 4 f, 37, 107
Eunomius, 69, 85
Euphranor, 52
Euphratio, 74
Eusebius of Caesarea, 36 f, 54, 68, 74 ff, 82, 90, 93 f, 121
Eusebius of Nicomedia, 69, 71, 73
Evans, E., 44 ff., 121

Fausset, W. L., 51 f
Festugière, A. J., 33, 119
Fitzmyer, J. A., 18
Frankfort, H., 108

Gaius, 80
Galen, 37
George of Laodicea, 54, 85 ff
Germinius, 80
Graef, H. C., 19
Grillmeier, A., 18, 121, 128

Harnack, A., 34
Harvey, cf. Ireneus
Hauret, C., 104
Hefele-Leclercq, 52, 54, 78
Heraclides, 50
Hermas, 19–22, 24, 26
Hessen, J., 11
Hilary, 23, 37, 55, 78 f, 90
Hippolytus, 36, 38 f, 41, 50 ff, 58, 111, 117, 122, 134
Holl, K., cf. Epiphanius
Homer, 116
Homoeans, 69, 76, 85, 87, 136
Homoeousians, 37, 69, 80, 85 ff, 94, 135
Huet, D., 65

Ignatius of Antioch, 19
Ireneus of Lyons, 19 f, 24, 30, 32, 111–16, 119 f, 122

Jaspers, K., 109
Jerome, 23, 55, 65, 80
Julius, Pope, 77
Justin, 23 f, 41, 120 f

Klostermann, E., cf. Eusebius of Caesarea, Marcellus of Ancyra
Koch, H., 63, 119, 126
Koetschau, cf. Origen
Kretschmar, G., 22
Kriebel, M., 46

Labbe, 75
Lebon, J., 92
Lebreton, J., 43
Leo XIII, xxii
Licinius, 73
Lietzmann, H., 92
Lonergan, B., ix–xxix, 2, 9, 16, 19, 94, 103, 127
Loofs, F., 37
Lucian of Antioch, 69, 71, 73, 76, 78

Malinine-Puech-Quispel, 27
Malinowski, B., 108
Maly, C. A., 81
Mandaeans, 33 f
Mani, Manicheans, 33 f
Marcellus of Ancyra, 54, 68, 76 ff, 81 f, 93 f
Marcion, 33 f
Maris of Chalcedon, 73
Maxwell, 103
McShane, P., xxv
Mendizábal, A., 31
Methodius, 66
Michaelis, W., 22
Musurillo, H., 56

Nautin, P., 38 f, 50 f
Nemeshegyi, P., 127

SUBJECT INDEX

Acacians, 80, 83
Adoptionists, xi, 8, 36 ff, 61
Allegory, 116–18
Anachronism, 41
Analogy, xii, xv, xxiii, 29 f, 34, 58, 60, 64, 78, 89, 102
Anthropomorphism, 71, 102, 110, 134 f
Archaism, 136
Arianism, Arians, xi, 8, 14, 53 f, 64, 66–74, 76 f, 79 ff, 84 f, 93, 95, 99, 105, 131, 134 f
Augustinian school, 6

Chalcedon, council of, xxvii, 92
Classicist view of culture, 106
Cognitional process, theory, xiv, 8
Common sense, 11; world of practical c.s., 109
Conceptualism, 56, 85
Consciousness, development of, 7, 16; divine c., xxiii; differentiation of c., 2 f, 6, 9, 109; patterns of c., 9 f; rational c., 60
Consubstantial, consubstantiality, xii, 9, 30 f, 34, 37, 40, 53, 60, 65 ff, 70–5, 86, 88–104, 128, 130 f, 135 f
Conversion, 7
Correspondence, truth and being, 85
Creed, Apostles', 71, 122, 127
Creeds of minor councils (340–60 A.D.), 78–84
Culture and cultural development, 4,

106 ff; Greek vs. Hebrew c., 108 ff; hellenistic c., xxvii, 33, 131; pagan c., 33, 119

Dialectic, 48 f, 59, 133; aristotelico-stoic d., 85; W. as functional specialty xxii, xxvii
Dialectical approach, xi; d. development, xi
Dogma, development of, emergence of, xi f, xviii, xxviii, 1–17
Dogmatic theologian, theology, xi f, 120 f

Eclecticism, 126
Epistemology and dogma, 8, 133
Essentialists, 10, 56
Exegesis, gnostic, 28, 32 f, 111 f; e. of Origen, 63, 125 ff development of e., 110–13

Faith, certitude of, xiii; preambles of f., 120; f. and reason, 120 f
Functional specialties in theology, xxii, xxiv, xxvi f

Gnostics, xi f, xxvii, 8, 18, 23, 26–35, 66, 89, 105, 111 ff, 116, 119, 122, 127, 130 f, 134
Good of order, particular g. and g. of value, 107 f
Greek philosophers, 115 ff
Greeks vs. Hebrews, 106, 108–10, 121; G. vs. Latins, 54, 87